READING THROUGH
EXODUS

WITH
THE DEVOTED COLLECTIVE

ᵗʰᵉ DEVOTED Collective

The Devoted Collective
Auckland, New Zealand
www.thedevotedcollective.org

ISBN Hardcover 978-0-473-67048-1

Typesetting by Holly Robertson of Design by Rocket www.designbyrocket.com
Illustrations by Marie Warner Preston of Outspoken Images www.outspokenimages.com
Edited by Vicki Bentley

Cataloguing in Publishing Data Title: Reading Through Exodus
Author: The Devoted Collective
Subjects: Devotions, Christian life, Spirituality

A copy of this title is held at the National Library of New Zealand

*In your unfailing love you will lead
the people you have redeemed.
In your strength you will guide them
to your holy dwelling.*

Exodus 15:13

Known in Hebrew as *Shemoth*, 'the book of names', from the opening line, Exodus reminds us that we serve a God who cares deeply about His people and knows them by name. This is no distant deity, but One who sees and hears and shows His concern by coming down and entering into it all *with us*. Yet He does more than simply journey alongside us, He calls us out—out of bondage and slavery to sin and into freedom, into relationship with Himself, inviting us to become a people who dwell in the beauty of His presence.

And so, we extend you the same invitation as we journey through Exodus together—to open yourself to the wonder of who He is and what He is leading you into. Each day, you'll read a portion of Scripture paired with a devotion designed to help you sink deep into the Word and reflect on God's goodness, mercy, sovereign power, as you marvel at the truth that a Holy God is calling you to Himself.

It is our prayer that these words enrich your understanding of His Word and strengthen your relationship with the One who has given His all for you to take your place in His family.

The Devoted Team

Contents

We Know

AIMÉE WALKER

Exodus 1

"But I didn't know. . ."

This is a common excuse in our household, and ignorance is frequently feigned when someone is confronted about something they actually *do* know they shouldn't have done. Their hope is that their lack of knowledge will somehow absolve them of responsibility and they will be able to escape the consequences of their actions.

As the story of Abraham's descendants resumes in the book of Exodus, we meet a thriving, increasing people who are filling the land of Egypt (v.7). With echoes of the creation account, we are reminded both that they are fulfilling God's purposes for them (Genesis 1:28), and that God has been faithful to His promise to Abraham to multiply his offspring (Genesis 15:5). Yet we're also being readied for the fulfilment of something else God had spoken to Abraham—for four hundred years, his descendants would be enslaved and mistreated in a foreign land (Genesis 15:13). A simple statement sets up the impending conflict for us: "Now there arose a new king over Egypt *who did not know* Joseph (v.8 ESV).

Pharaoh did not know.

He didn't know how Joseph had served his predecessors. He didn't know how Joseph had served the nation, saving them from starvation while a famine raged. He didn't know that his family had been welcomed in and given land as a token of Egypt's gratitude. *He didn't know. . .* and this lack of knowledge shaped his behaviour causing him to fear the very people who were meant to be a blessing to him.

Lack of knowledge and fear is a toxic combination, and we see its consequences playing out in the opening verses of Exodus where, enslaved and oppressed, the Israelites are worked ruthlessly. But the more they are oppressed, the more they multiply, and the more they multiply, the more the Egyptians dread them. In a desperate attempt to regain control and subdue them, Pharaoh does something unimaginable, issuing instructions to the Hebrew midwives that any boy they deliver must be killed. Only the girls can be allowed to live.

However, the Hebrew midwives know something that Pharaoh doesn't. They know the Lord, and their fear is of Him alone. Just as Pharaoh's lack of knowledge shaped his behaviour, their understanding of God and His ways shapes theirs, and they allow the boys to live. Scripture repeatedly promises us that our fear of the Lord brings a blessing, and in this case, God rewards their obedience by giving them each children of their own (v.21).

But a deeper conflict underlies this story and our own—a conflict that continues to this day. There is an enemy who *does* know the Lord, who understands the threat that God's people pose to his dominion and authority in this world, and who has been bent on our destruction since the Garden of Eden. Like the Hebrew midwives Shiphrah and Puah, this reality requires us to determine what we know and believe to be true, and ultimately decide who *we* will fear.

Will we live afraid of what our enemy can do to us, or, will we allow the fear of the Lord to shape our lives?

God's faithfulness and redemptive power is on full display throughout this first chapter. We see that He can be trusted to keep His Word and to fulfil what He has promised. No matter what weapon the enemy wields against His people, it cannot prosper, and time and again, He turns what was meant for their destruction to be for their good and His glory. And we can be confident that all of this still holds true today. Even as we live under leaders who do not know the Lord, who oppress the Truth and persecute our faith, we can be assured that God has not forgotten His people. He can be trusted to build His Church—a fruitful, increasing, body of people who cannot be constrained—and to make all things new.

We know something even the Israelites didn't fully know back then: We know the end of the story. And friends, that should change everything. *We know.* May it fill us with a holy boldness to pursue God's purposes for our generation and to obey Him alone.

As we begin our journey with the Israelites, what truths about God and His purposes do you need to remind yourself of? Turn them into "I know..." statements and as you declare them aloud invite Holy Spirit to empower you to walk in the fear of the Lord.

Drawn Out

KAY GLEAVES

Exodus 2

I don't remember my time as a baby. I mean, no one does, *right?* That doesn't mean it's not a part of my story. The fact is, things happened in my life when I was a baby that dramatically shaped my life: a divorce, a fight for custody, a new family, gang violence, and an alcohol and drug-riddled environment. Honestly, I'm glad I can't remember it all.

Maybe Moses is glad he can't remember being placed in a basket in the Nile River either, but it still happened. It's still a part of his story. And it set in motion a greater story that would lead to freedom and redemption for many. I see this in Moses' life, and I also see it in mine.

In Exodus 2, from the water of the river to the water at a well, we see not only Moses' story unfold, but also God's redemption story for all of Israel. With that in mind, these details stand out to me about Moses' early life: Born a Levite, Moses was of the priestly tribe—from birth, he had God-given destiny and responsibility. Yes, Moses was special. His mother saw it, and not just because she was his mum, but because she knew he had a purpose for which he must be saved. Her actions proved she trusted God. Putting him in a basket wasn't a last act of desperation; it was a faithful act of a woman who knew her child was created for something special.

Moses' name means 'I drew him out of the water'. An Egyptian princess may have spoken his name on earth, but the truth is, God called it out before the foundations of the world. God drew him out of the water for a purpose even greater than this princess could have ever imagined. And it's not lost on me that after Moses killed an Egyptian and fled for his life, he again landed by water, sitting down by a well. God was about to draw him out again.

Moses was a "sojourner in a foreign land" (Exodus 2:22 ESV). He was able to look back on his story thus far and realize he had been residing temporarily in a place that was not his own. He acknowledged his position and place as one of belonging, but also recognised the parts of his story that got him there.

Moses' life encourages me to again contemplate my own story and view it through the lens of God's story too. A story of freedom and redemption with the resounding awareness that I was made for a purpose, on purpose. None of it was wasted, and, like Moses, there is so much still to come.

Verses 23-25 are perhaps my most favourite part of this chapter. They don't just show us Moses, they show us God:

God hears.

God sees.

God remembers.

God knew.

God understood.

Isn't that the best part of our stories?

Through it all—when we're thrown into rivers in our own 'proverbial baskets', caught in sins, shamed by mistakes, on the run, seen as strangers, trying to adapt and change, making new lives, or however else our own personal stories would have us fill in those blanks— God isn't absent. Though varied and different, our stories are never ours alone. There's a God-story woven through it all, and He hears, sees, remembers, knows, and understands all the places we've been sojourning.

I love that this chapter ends with a holy building of anticipation for what is to come for Moses. May we, too, see our stories with that same holy anticipation. God's up to something, friends. He started a story in us, He hasn't abandoned us in it, and He will see it through to its holy completion.

Take some time to reflect on your own story:
How does viewing it through the lens of God's
story shift your perspective? Where do you need
to be reminded that He is still with you and will
see what He has started through to completion?

_____

_____

_____

_____

_____

_____

_____

_____

_____

_____

_____

_____

_____

_____

_____

_____

_____

_____

_____

_____

_____

Holy Ground

MAZHAR KEFALI

Exodus 3

As we enter this season of Moses' life, we find him working as a shepherd to his father-in-law's flock. Now eighty years old, he has spent the past forty years in relative obscurity and long periods of solitude in the desert.

One day, as he tends to the sheep near Mount Horeb (also called Sinai) he has an experience that alters the trajectory of his life and sets him on a pathway that changes history: he encounters a burning bush in which Yahweh speaks to him.

As Moses approaches the burning bush, Yahweh's first words establish the nature of the encounter—one that is holy and requires an approach of utter humility and reverence. He tells Moses not to get any closer and to remove his sandals for he is now standing on "holy ground" (v.5).

It was customary at the time, and still is in many cultures today, to take your shoes off when entering a home as a sign of respect, especially in the presence of nobility. Here, the ground was holy, not because of anything inherently pure in it, but because of God's presence. He *is* absolute holiness and wherever His presence is manifest, we are on holy ground. Therefore we must always encounter Him as He prescribes—humbly and reverently.

Yahweh reveals to Moses that for the past forty years He has not been a distant, uncaring God, rather He informs Moses of His heart and intentions concerning His people. He has "seen the misery. . . heard them crying out. . . [been] concerned for their suffering" and "the cry of the Israelites [has] reached [Him]" (vv.7-9).

In response, He tells Moses He is going to "come down" and intervene, in order to deliver His people from slavery into a new land that is "good and spacious" (v.8).

He then drops the bombshell on Moses: "So now, go, I am sending you. . . " (v.10). One can only imagine Moses' response. A Q&A follows as Moses seeks to wrap his head around all that is taking place. His response is not one of rebellion, but one of humble inadequacy. He once tried to be his people's deliverer back in Egypt, but failed miserably and had to flee to safety. Forty years later he is being assigned the same task, but now he is a more humbled, broken, and prepared man. When we realise we are too weak to lead, we find ourselves better prepared for the calling ahead of us. This necessary preparation of our character gives us the capacity to steward His purposes without imploding under the weight of the responsibility that comes with serving Him.

Moses then asks a key question: If the Israelites ask who has sent me, "what shall I tell them?" (v.13). God reveals His name and nature in His answer 'Yahweh'—the most revered name of God to His people. The essential meaning is: 'I am who I am, existing eternally'. He is completely self-existent and self-sufficient in Himself.

The significance in knowing the name of deity in ancient culture was twofold. Firstly, the name revealed the nature and attributes of God Himself. Secondly, He was defining His relationship to His people as a relational God, a covenant keeping God, as "the God of your fathers. . . " (v.15). This is no distant deity but One who binds Himself in covenant relationship to His people, giving them confidence that He will fulfil all He has promised them.

Yahweh gives Moses one key sign in response to his questions about who He is and what He is asking him to do: His delivered, redeemed people would one day "worship" Him on this very mountain (v.12). This sign still identifies the people of God today who have received His mercy: "But you are a chosen people, a royal priesthood, a holy nation, a people belonging to God, that you may declare the praises of Him who called you out of darkness into His wonderful light" (1 Peter 2:9-10). Whatever 'holy ground' we may be standing on today, let us worship in the presence of the great I AM with humble reverence and awe, fully assured of His faithful and enduring care and provision for us, His dearly-loved children.

What holy ground do you find yourself standing on in this season? How is God revealing Himself to you there and what is He inviting you to do in response?

_____

_____

_____

_____

_____

_____

_____

_____

_____

_____

_____

_____

_____

_____

_____

_____

_____

_____

_____

_____

_____

DAY FOUR
Consecrated
PAULA MORRISON

Exodus 4

When I was a young child, I used to run off quite a lot with just a packed lunch and my cat for company. I blame Enid Blyton and her tales of the *Famous Five* adventurers. I would disappear for a whole day until I heard my mum calling me for dinner in the distance and reluctantly made the long trek home—more scared of my mother (and rightly so!) than anything out there in the big wide world.

In this chapter we see Moses' fear of the people he would encounter on the mission God had given him. His mind immediately goes to everything that could possibly go wrong: "What if they do not believe me or listen to me?" (v.1).

Honestly, I understand why Moses runs when God first turns his staff into a snake—I am not a big fan of snakes either. However, the act is a symbolic one. Moses' staff represents his authority and the serpent points to Pharaoh—his cobra headdress a symbol for the goddess Wadget who Pharaoh relies on for protection. Moses is clearly afraid of Pharaoh, in fact he fears Pharaoh more than the God of the universe. Yet, when Moses picks up the snake it turns back into his staff, a clear demonstration it is God who is in charge—and the One who should be feared (Proverbs 9:10). God then gives Moses a second sign emphasising the contrast between the hand of Moses and the hand of God—the latter by which all things will be accomplished. Yet even though Moses had all the symbolism he needed that God was with him, the excuses kept coming.

Have you ever been tempted to run away and offer excuses when God is asking you to step forward in faith? I know I have. I, too, have asked: "Is there no one else?" I confess like Moses to saying I am not eloquent enough to speak. What a comfort it is to those of us who feel this way to know that our faithful God will help us to speak and teach us what to say when we put our trust in Him (vv.11-12).

As Moses starts the journey back to Egypt he is riding on a donkey with the staff of God in his hand. Moses has been equipped to deliver the Israelites from bondage, and this image is a foreshadowing of Jesus who will one day ride on a donkey into Jerusalem to deliver the world from their bondage of sin. However, the chapter doesn't end with this triumphant entry. We read in verse 24 that, shockingly, the Lord is about to kill Moses.

Ironically, Moses has been afraid of Pharaoh and the Israelites this whole time, but really his fear should have been directed towards God as he had neglected to have his son circumcised as the law commanded. Moses' life was spared by his wife Zipporah, who carried out the required shedding of blood and parting of flesh. Just as it was for Moses under the Old Covenant, a body that is pleasing to Jesus today is a body that is consecrated to Him. As believers, our bodies belong to Jesus. As Paul urges believers in Romans 12:1: "in view of God's mercy. . . offer your bodies as a living sacrifice, holy and pleasing to God—this is your true and proper worship."

Just as it was right for me to respect and obey my mother as a child, may we, too, fear God rightly and obey Him completely in body, mind, and spirit. We need not fear anything else. As David prayed in Psalm 34: "I sought the Lord and he answered me; he delivered me from all my fears. . . fear the Lord, you his holy people, for those who fear Him lack nothing" (vv.4 and 9).

How is God inviting you to offer your body as a living sacrifice in this season? What fears are holding you back from being all in? Bring them honestly before Him and ask Holy Spirit to instead give you a spirit of love, power, and sound mind with which to serve the Lord.

_____
_____
_____
_____
_____
_____
_____
_____
_____
_____
_____
_____
_____
_____
_____
_____
_____
_____
_____
_____
_____
_____
_____

DAY FIVE
God's Not Finished Yet
SHELLEY JOHNSON

Exodus 5

When the call to move came in the summer of 2020, I had complete confidence that God's hand was in it and believed with certainty He would provide everything we needed—including a new job for me. I dutifully applied to women's ministries, excited to see which door He would open. My certainty pushed me onward, but it also created assumptions about God's plans.

When Moses comes before Pharaoh at this first meeting in Exodus 5, I picture him stepping forward with a similar assurance. By this point, God has answered Moses' concerns about taking on this leadership role and has performed miracles to prove His word is true. Moses and Aaron's confidence appears justified then as they boldly tell the king of Egypt that, "the Lord, the God of Israel says, 'Let my people go'" (v.1).

The proverbial gauntlet is thrown down. Expectations are surely high that God will fulfil all He has promised.

I can easily imagine Moses' concern when Pharaoh pridefully refuses to listen to a god he's never heard of (v.2). To be fair, God had warned Moses that Pharaoh would not let the Israelites go unless a "mighty hand" compelled him (Exodus 3:19), so this resistance should not have been wholly unexpected.

With this in mind, Moses moves forward. Determined to sway Pharaoh, Moses and Aaron repeat the command, suggesting that God may even punish the Israelites if the request is not granted (v.3).

Ironically, instead of releasing them, Pharaoh doles out his own consequence to his slaves—no straw for bricks without a change in quotas (vv.7-8).

Not surprisingly, the brick supply drops and the Israelites are beaten. When they confront Moses with anger and judgement (v.21), he wonders what has gone wrong—there had been no warning of such brutality. Moses' certainty fades with confusion; what he had expected of God has not come to pass. In fact, Moses' actions have had the opposite impact, and his people now face harsher circumstances than ever before. Frustrated, Moses confronts God, "Why have you brought trouble upon this people? Is this why you sent me?" (v.22).

I feel the weight of the frustration Moses carries. He has obeyed God—so where is He?

For a year I waited, and the door to a new job remained firmly closed. I constantly looked to God with Moses-like questions, *Why have You brought me here to do nothing? Is this all You have for me—this confusion and loneliness?*

Like Moses, I didn't understand why God wasn't doing what I had assumed He would. But, unlike Moses, I know how *his* story ends. I know God comes through for him. In fact, I know the story of Exodus has only just begun. But, in this scene, Moses does not know the ending. He only sees what's right in front of him.

Still, he doesn't give up. He goes to God with his dashed expectations, inspiring me to do the same. Moses' assumptions about God helps me to check my own and to remain open to what God has in mind, because His ways are higher than mine (Isaiah 55:9). And as I observe Moses at this point in his story, I'm reminded that God is not finished yet—not with Moses, not with me, and certainly not with you.

Wherever you find yourself in your story, know that the Author and Perfecter of your faith is still at work (Hebrews 12:2). If circumstances seem worse for your obedience or your trust in God, think of Moses and keep going to God for the assurance that He remains with you, He will never forsake you, and He always finishes the work He has begun (Philippians 1:6).

Where in your life have you been putting God in a box? What does it look like for you to take the lid off and trust His ways? Invite Holy Spirit to help you wait on the Lord well.

DAY SIX

Rock Bottom

ASHLEY KELLY

Exodus 6

"Hitting rock bottom" is an expression that doesn't require much explanation. We read books about characters who slam into it hard and fast. We watch movies and TV shows filled with storylines that illustrate in full colour what it looks like to plummet headfirst towards it. Our news cycles and social media feeds thrive on the tragedy of it in the lives of the rich and famous. And perhaps we have even experienced it ourselves, whether in our own lives or that of a loved one.

Thinking about the hundreds of years the Israelites endured slavery, harsh treatment, and cruel work conditions, it's hard to imagine that life could get much worse. But it does. Perhaps what makes it exceptionally painful is the fact that their rock bottom comes after a glimmer of life-changing hope.

Moses has already entered the scene. He has already proclaimed God is going to set them free. Things are looking up for the people of God. Hope, like the early morning sunrise, is peeking above the horizon, promising a day full of light and gently warming their outlook for the future.

It is in the midst of this newly soaring hope that they suddenly and unexpectedly find themselves flat on their backs with their breath knocked out of them. Pharaoh refuses Moses' plea to let them go. He enforces heavier labour upon them, requiring more effort from them. The Israelites are hitting rock bottom, and, for them, the bottom is bricks, bricks, and more bricks.

Pharaoh does not free the Israelites, so he clearly isn't their saviour. The people of God are overwhelmed and overworked, so they can't possibly save themselves. Even Moses isn't able to accomplish the goal. Yet, when Moses calls out to God, failure in his voice, God makes it very clear *who* is going to be doing the saving. "I am the Lord, and I will bring you out from under the burdens of the Egyptians, and I will deliver you from slavery to them, and I will. . . I will. . . I will. . . " (v.6 ESV). God will do it. God, alone, will do the saving!

But we can't forget about the whole rock-bottom situation the Iraelites are experiencing. They can't forget it either. In fact, "they did not listen to Moses because of their broken spirit and harsh slavery" (v.9 ESV). Their hopes had already been sparked, and it nearly crushed them. Their "broken spirit" speaks to the idea of their very breath being knocked out of them. Breath often equates to life, which leads us to the conclusion that they have nothing left. No fight. No hope. No breath.

Here's the beauty in this raw and honest depiction of the Israelites: Their deliverance from Egypt is not dependent on how they feel or even what they believe. Remember, God has already and definitively proclaimed that *He will* deliver them, that *He will* do it. If the Israelites aren't powerful enough to save themselves, then they sure aren't powerful enough to hinder God from saving them. It's not up to them. It's all up to God!

They can't listen to Moses. They can't find the strength to get their hopes up again. They are at rock bottom with no way to save themselves. And that is exactly where God wants them. For He is about to enter into their absolute weakness, brokenness, and hopelessness with His mighty arm to save and free His people.

Rock bottom hurts. Weakness and inability hurt. But as the Israelites will soon learn, and as the Apostle Paul teaches us in the New Testament, it is for our benefit that we learn to become "content with weaknesses, insults, hardships, persecutions, and calamities" (2 Corinthians 12:10 ESV). It is then, in our weakness, that we are truly strong—not in our own ability, of course, but in God who says: "My grace is sufficient for you, for my power is made perfect in weakness" (2 Corinthians 12:9 ESV).

Where do you feel like the breath has been knocked out of you? Get specific and make Paul's words your own, declaring: God Your grace is sufficient for me. Your power is made perfect in. . .

Wannabe Gods

VICKI BENTLEY

Exodus 7

"Don't settle for less than God's best."

It's a phrase I've heard often over the years, and it's the first one that comes to mind as we turn to this chapter of Exodus and witness a fascinating face-off between God and the wannabe god that is Pharaoh.

Pharaoh's disdain for God is already evident in his arrogant and disrespectful question in Exodus 5:2: "Who is the Lord, that I should obey him and let Israel go?" In response, God seeks to show Pharaoh exactly who he is dealing with through a miracle performed through His servant Aaron's staff (v.10).

However, instead of being humbled by the sight of the staff turning into a snake before his eyes, Pharaoh chooses to call in his own group of 'fakes'—"the magicians of Egypt"—who replicate the act with their occult magic (v.11). Even though Aaron's staff swallows up the others, reinforcing the ultimate power of God over these poor substitutes, Pharaoh's heart is hardened against God (v.13).

In response to Pharaoh's stubborn refusal to yield to God's will, Moses is tasked with delivering the first plague of blood to the Egyptians along with a message from God: "by this you will know that I am the Lord" (v.17). Yet even as rivers turn crimson, the fish die, and the Egyptians thirst, we read that "the magicians of Egypt used their magic, and they, too, turned water into blood. So Pharaoh's heart remained hard" (v.22 NLT).

Using their dark arts, the magicians again found a way to replicate God's miracle. But interestingly, they didn't turn the blood *back* to water—I imagine because they couldn't. This was an act that only the Creator could do; an act that trumped not only the magicians but the god of the Nile, a 'deity' worshipped by the Egyptians. Pharaoh, however, was undeterred. He "turned and went into his palace, and did not take even this to heart" (v.23).

Evidently Pharaoh could not see the true God for the gods he had surrounded himself with. Prepared to settle for poor substitutes over the Sovereign—the only One who could truly save his soul, and his people—the consequences would be dire for them all.

While we may shake our heads at Pharaoh's foolishness, I wonder if sometimes we are guilty of the same kind of ignorance. As Paul writes in 2 Corinthians 11:3, "But I fear that somehow your pure and undivided devotion to Christ will be corrupted. . . just as Eve was deceived by the cunning ways of the serpent" (NLT).

How often do we settle for something the world offers because it seems better or equal to what God promises us? The enemy knows our weak spots and he, too, offers us fakes—idols that conjure up feelings of fulfilment, happiness, even worship. Yet at the end of the day they leave us empty and wanting, a far cry from the full and abundant life we could have in Christ—the only true source of joy, peace, and hope.

As we reflect on this passage, perhaps we, too, should consider the attitude of our own hearts towards our Creator. For if we allow ourselves to be blinded by the world and its secular substitutes—obstructing the truth of who God is and offering us little by way of comparison—God may choose to give us over to our false idols, hardening our distracted hearts like Pharaoh and causing us to turn away from Him for good.

"[God] is the only true God, and he is eternal life" (1 John 5:20b NLT). So let's elevate Him to His rightful place in our hearts and remove any false idols that try to claim our fidelity for themselves. "There is no one holy like the Lord," after all (1 Samuel 2:2), and we should never settle for less.

Where have you been tempted to settle for less than God's best? What does it look like for you to elevate God and put Him first?

DAY EIGHT
Tomorrow
EMILY TYLER

Exodus 8

A few years back I had the unfortunate experience of encountering hundreds of maggots wriggling and crawling all over my front door. They were not only on the door, but the infestation also continued to the doorstep, up the garden path, and even on the back of the car. Swinging into action, I ran into the house like a mad woman, boiled the kettle, grabbed the bleach, and donned my rubber gloves. I set to work immediately. Nothing was going to stop me from doing whatever I could to rid my home of these horrific creatures.

The next three plagues we read about in Exodus 8 were not confined to the front door either! Frogs and insects were everywhere. . . in beds, ovens, mixing bowls, even on the people and animals.

When God multiplied the frogs, He was giving the Egyptians more of what they worshipped. Frogs were believed to be part of two worlds; they were considered sacred and couldn't be killed. Even the Egyptian goddess Heqet was pictured with a frog's head. But too much of a good thing reeks (v.14) when it replaces God's position as sovereign in our lives. Their beloved frogs, a respected element of their paganism, became a curse instead of a blessing as the Egyptians were forced to loathe the very symbol of their wicked worship.

Understandably, recognising that his magicians could only make the matter worse by multiplying the frogs rather than banishing them, Pharaoh reaches breaking point. He summons Moses and Aaron and says, "Pray to the Lord to take the frogs away from me and my people, and I will let your people go to offer sacrifices to the Lord" (v.8). Pharaoh seemingly repents and promises the Israelites' release.

In his kindness, Moses gives Pharaoh the option to choose *when* to have the frogs removed. If someone had offered to take away my maggots, I would have said, "Immediately, don't wait!" Yet he says, "Tomorrow" (v.10). Incessantly croaking, slimy, hopping frogs were everywhere.

Tomorrow, really?

And yet, it dawns on me that I am no different than Pharaoh. The idols established in my life sometimes remain until 'tomorrow'. *Forgiving someone?* I'll do it—*after* they apologise first. *Laying down my pride, anger, or lust?* I'll do it tomorrow. *Releasing funds as an offering?* After the paycheck comes in. *Making healthy choices to honour my body?* The diet starts tomorrow. . .

If our sin looked as gross to us as a maggot infestation we wouldn't be waiting until tomorrow. Instead, we straddle two froggy worlds trying to worship people and things rather than God. Like Pharaoh, we may feel remorse and want relief from the consequences of our sin but without the commitment to repent. Yet true repentance doesn't wait until tomorrow, it begins now.

Repentance is total surrender to God and not something we can fake as Pharaoh discovered. He relented when he regretted the frogs' presence, but then immediately chose to harden his heart the moment relief came. The respite removed any remorse, and with it, his resolve to repent. Sadly many of us will be familiar with calling out to God in the middle of a crisis only to relegate Him when the pressure is removed. Pharaoh thought *he* was in control, but as soon as he reneged on his promise the third plague came without warning. We might choose sin, but we can't choose the consequences.

God sent Moses to deliver the Israelites from physical slavery, and He sent Jesus to deliver us from slavery to sin (John 8:24). On the cross He did all that was necessary to rid the world of sin's infestation, declaring to Satan, sin, and death: "Let my people go" (Exodus 8:1). Just as Moses was commanded to stand in Pharaoh's presence and not bow as custom demanded, we too can stand boldly in the knowledge that we have been completely set free from guilt, shame, and condemnation, and have ultimate victory over sin and the grave.

Benjamin Franklin said, "Don't put off till tomorrow what you can do today." Don't wait till tomorrow, friends. You are free in Christ—today.

Allow Holy Spirit to reveal anything you have been procrastinating or leaving until 'tomorrow'. Ask the Lord to energise you afresh to arise and complete the tasks He has assigned for you to do. Commit to being quick to obey His promptings today.

Hard Hearts

AIMÉE WALKER

Exodus 9

My grandfather was a keen gardener. Growing up, whenever we visited their home, he would proudly take us to see his garden, always pointing out in his thick Turkish accent how well his beloved 'caspicums' were doing. Everything he planted thrived, not solely due to his dilligent care, but also because of the environment—the ground where they lived was rich volcanic soil, providing optimal conditions for growth.

In the gospels, Jesus tells a parable about a farmer who went out to sow seed in his fields. As he scatters the seed, some falls along the path where the birds come and eat it before it can germinate; other seed falls in rocky places where the soil lacks the depth for it to fully take root, and some falls among the thorns where, while it grows, the weeds choke out its fruitfulness. But the rest falls in good soil where it is able to take root and produce a crop up to a hundred times greater than what was initially sown (Matthew 13:9). When He later explains the meaning to the disciples, Jesus makes it abundantly clear how important its message is—in fact, He tells them that understanding this parable is the key to understanding all the other parables (Mark 4:13). *Why?* Because it is about how willing we are to receive and respond to the Word of God and the message of the Kingdom. Good soil, Jesus tells us, represents those "with a noble and good heart, who hear the word, retain it, and by persevering produce a crop" (Luke 8:15).

It might seem funny to segue from the plagues of Exodus into this New Testament parable, but as I studied this chapter and the ones that precede it, I couldn't help but notice a recurring theme: God speaks, and the people—in particular, Pharaoh—have a choice as to how they will respond. Over and over we read the phrase, "Then the Lord said," and over and over we see that Pharaoh not only refuses to listen, but five times he also hardens his heart. And like the seed that was unable to take root, Moses' message from God, was unable to penetrate Pharaoh's obstinate heart.

There are two primary words used to describe Pharaoh's hardness of heart: *kābad* and *ḥāzaq*. Each of these words carries both positive and negative connotations, but in this instance, there is nothing good to be said about the condition of his 'soil'. It is dull and unresponsive—*kābad*—to God's instructions, and the longer the plagues continue, the more rigid and unyielding—*ḥāzaq*—he becomes in his position. And so, he, and those officials who also chose to harden their hearts, miss out on the opportunity God offers them for reprieve from the full impact of the sixth plague; only those who revered the Word of the Lord and acted upon it avoided death and received this act of grace (vv.20-21).

However, in spite of this hardness of heart, and even because of it, God's purposes ultimately prevail. As God triumphs over the Egyptian gods and rulers, it is clear that there is no one like Him (v.14). His power is made evident, and His name is proclaimed in all the earth (v.16).

Without fail, God does what He says He will (vv.5-6), and His Word never returns to Him empty—it always fulfils the purpose He has for it (Isaiah 55:11). But if we want to receive the grace of what He speaks and see His Word yield a fruitful harvest in our lives, we are wise to check the soil of our own hearts. As we consider Pharaoh's choices in parallel with the parable Jesus shared, it's easy to think in terms of categories of people who have four distinct responses to the Word—and if we've received Christ as Lord, we can tend to exclude ourselves from its lesson, viewing ourselves only as the good soil. But even though I've said "yes" to Jesus, I've learned my heart is capable of all of these responses to God's Word. And that means I, too, can be the hard, unyielding soil.

Yet just as God gave the Eqyptians an opportunity to know grace, He continually offers us the same, giving us the gift of Holy Spirit to till our soil, breaking up the hard places and making our hearts fertile ground so that God might fulfil His purposes in partnership *with* us rather than in spite of us.

How do you see your own heart reflected in the four types of soil Jesus identified in the Parable of the Sower? Is there anywhere you need to repent and invite Holy Spirit to soften the soil of your heart?

DAY TEN
Illuminate the Way
ADÉLE DEYSEL

Exodus 10

Have you ever been stuck in the dark?

As a teenager, I visited the Cango Caves in South Africa during a school tour. Sitting in one of the impressive twenty-six chambers, I vividly remember the moment the lights were switched off—total darkness! My eyes could not adjust to the lack of light, and the acoustics of the room amplified every voice into an overwhelming echo. Although surrounded by people, I felt alone, trapped, scared, and disorientated.

I 'felt' the darkness that day.

In this passage of Exodus, the Egyptians are plunged into total darkness for seventy-two hours—a darkness so thick it "can be felt" (v.21). The Israelites, however, continue to have light (v.23). Throughout the Bible, darkness is associated with God's abandonment and judgement, representing hopelessness and death. But darkness became powerless when God created light (Genesis 1:3). The only way to fight darkness is with the presence of light, and the only light that cannot be extinguished is God!

This plague was a powerful symbol as the Egyptians believed that Ra—the sun god—ruled over the earth, sky, and underworld, and appeared each day as the noon-day sun. By extinguishing this light source, the God of Israel demonstrated His power over creation, life, and death. Egyptian gods were once again proven powerless compared to Yahweh, the God of Israel.

Isolated in their thoughts and unable to see beyond the darkness, the Egyptians would have gravely questioned their identity, as I have done many times myself. Each time I felt as though the darkness that consumed my mind was so profound that living in God's light felt unobtainable.

Light gives our brains the ability to process images, therefore its presence makes sight possible. We can only fight the darkness in our minds with God's light (1 John 1:15)! Reading and studying the Word of God equips us to fight the darkness that wants to consume us; it is a lamp for our feet and gives light to our path (Psalm 119:105). His Word *is* the light we need when darkness overwhelms us.

Seven times now God's ultimatum remains unchanged: "Let my people go!" But Pharaoh persistently tries to negotiate. Darkness for the Egyptians might have ended but Pharaoh remains lost in the isolation of his darkened heart, yet to learn that God does not negotiate! God fiercely wants His people to be fully freed from the bondage of slavery—including all of their possessions.

I have tried negotiating the terms of my own surrender with God, attempting to retain control of certain areas of my life. It was my inability to understand God's love and grace that limited my own submission. God wants us to be fully free and gave us Jesus to prove His love. He wants full surrender so that we can live in the light that He alone provides.

Jesus stepped down from glory to meet us in our darkness. And He knows well its heaviness—abandoned in His final moments, darkness covered the earth as God withdrew (Matthew 27:46). But three days later, the light pierced through that darkness forever when Jesus rose from the dead. The ultimate price for sin had been paid, giving us eternal access to God.

Waiting in darkness and living our lives in the isolation and chains of sinful habits and faulty thinking patterns will leave us feeling hopeless; it may even cause us to believe that God has withdrawn from our lives. Yet as God's people we have been given authority over darkness in the name of Jesus.

Let's choose full surrender and live confidently in the light of the One who created it, with the assurance that "whoever follows [Him] will never walk in darkness, but will have the light of life" (John 8:12).

Where in your life do you feel like the darkness is winning? Invite Holy Spirit to illuminate the path forward. What is one way you sense He is showing you how to take authority and bring the light and hope of Jesus to that place?

_____

_____

_____

_____

_____

_____

_____

_____

_____

_____

_____

_____

_____

_____

_____

_____

_____

_____

_____

_____

_____

_____

_____

A *Distinct People*

SHELLEY JOHNSON

Exodus 11

At the time of Joseph's rule in Egypt, Pharaoh settled God's people in an area called Goshen (Genesis 46). This region along the eastern edges of the Nile, bordering the Promised Land, gave the Hebrew people a land far removed from the cultish Egyptians to raise their herds. Considered 'detestable shepherds' by their neighbours (Genesis 46:34), the Hebrew people were left to themselves for centuries to grow and flourish (Genesis 47:27).

When we revisit the Israelites in Moses' day, they have grown in number to 600,000 men, plus women and children (Exodus 12:37). Though they remain in Goshen, boundaries have faded and God's people no longer inhabit the land alone. Yet, the Israelites remain set apart spiritually—distinct from their Egyptian neighbours in their worship of the One True God.

To further stress this reality, when God delivers his final speech to Pharaoh through His servant Moses, He makes "a distinction between Egypt and Israel" (v.7), declaring that the tenth and final plague will be so devastating that the wailing throughout Egypt will be "worse than there has ever been or ever will be again" (v.6). In contrast to the loud cries of grief in Egypt, absolute silence will cover the people of Israel—so quiet, in fact, that not even a dog will bark (v.7).

The devastating loss that will plague Egypt will not fall upon God's people. With the death of every firstborn in Egypt, the separation between believer and unbeliever will be complete. And Israel will be sent out at last.

As God's people today, we no longer inhabit our own land or exist as our own nation. Instead, Christians reside among neighbours who follow others gods and worship idols, seen and unseen. We dwell as scattered people among all nations, yet we are called to be "set apart as holy" unto the Lord (2 Timothy 2:21 ESV).

For Moses and the Israelites, living as sanctified people meant denying the gods and rituals of Egypt. It looked like refusing Pharaoh's decree to kill babies as they were born (Exodus 1:17). It looked like standing up against an emperor who saw himself as higher than God (Exodus 5:2). It looked like trusting one God above all other gods for deliverance from captivity.

For Christians today, living set apart means denying the idols of power and wealth and fame that permeate our culture. It looks like refusing to be conformed by the world and instead being transformed by the renewing of our minds (Romans 12:2). It looks like taking a stand for what is right even if everyone else insults and persecutes us for it. It looks like trusting our Saviour to continue His work of salvation in us and around us (Philippians 2:12).

Personally, I have struggled to live in the world while not succumbing to its ways. My preference is to hide away in my home in order to avoid the divisiveness and ridicule that my faith brings, or blend in to avoid making waves among people. Neither option is the way I'm called to live. I am meant to engage people—to live *in* the world but not be *of* it (John 17:16). Most days, then, I find myself needing to sit with God and remember my call to go out and love my neighbours as myself (Matthew 22:39).

God makes a clear distinction between His people and the rest of the world. If we're to be known as God's people, we must make an intentional choice each day to live holy lives—set apart in Christ, for Christ. And, as we do, people will know who we are—and who He is—by our love (John 13:35).

Is there any way in which you have succumbed to worldly culture? Invite Holy Spirit to renew your mind and to show you how to live set apart for God in that place.

DAY TWELVE
Remember This
KAY GLEAVES

Exodus 12

I think this just became my favourite chapter in the Bible. I have read several devotions on the subject of Passover and how it relates to the blood of Christ but it was only recently when I was doing my own study of this passage, that I truly understood for the first time its correlation not just to Christ's blood shed on the cross, but also to communion as a whole. The meaning of the unleavened bread and blood-covered doorposts finally hit home for me and unlocked an entirely new promise.

With the final plague looming, the Lord gives the Israelites instructions on how to prepare the lamb and unleavened bread (vv.1-20). This is followed by explicit and important instructions from Moses on how and why the blood should be put on the doorposts (vv.21-27). The Israelites do all that is commanded, and in verses 28-32 we see the retribution of the Lord as He passes over the doorposts—the event that leads to the long-awaited exodus of His children (vv.33-41).

By now, the children of Israel have been in captivity for four hundred and thirty years. Yet, in Psalm 105:37 we read, "He brought them forth also with silver and gold and there was not one feeble among their tribes" (KJV). Think about it! An estimated two million people endured four hundred and thirty years of slavery—captivity, back-breaking labour, and poor living conditions—and not one was feeble. Four hundred and thirty years of slavery must have brought about some injuries, some illness, some weakness. Yet not one was weak; not one faltered; not one stumbled. Not *one* in two million!

It's hard to imagine, isn't it? I don't know how I missed it before in all my reading and studying of this chapter, but that's a miracle. I have goosebumps just thinking about it.

One night of sacrifice, blood, bread, obedience, and sacrifice. One

43

swoop of power, presence, protection, promise, and purpose. And over two million people walked out of captivity—free, radically rich, healed, and protected. And it leads me to contemplate:

What Egypt do I need to escape from?

Where am I feeble?

What makes me stumble?

When do I falter?

And, most importantly, have I missed the full power of communion in my own life?

The Israelites are instructed a few times throughout this passage to: 'remember this', 'put it on the calendar', 'write it down', 'set a marker', 'tell your children', 'make this a practice'. And I think that message is also for us today. The God of yesterday, today, and forever wants us to be free; He wants us to be radically blessed, healed, and protected too!

I love this redemption story. I love the preparation, the promise, and the power. So as we partake in the act of remembrance that is communion, let's remember it, practice it, but also believe in the promise He has given us. Just like the children of Israel, we can leave our 'Egypt's' behind us, whatever they might be, with the full power, presence, protection, promise, and purpose of God with us and before us every step of the way.

Carve out some time today to take communion and remember God's activity in your own life. As you ponder all that Christ has brought you out of, where do you still need to experience freedom and healing? Bring it before the Lord and allow His past faithfulness to fuel fresh expectation for what lies ahead.

The Best Way

EMILY TYLER

Exodus 13

Several years ago, my husband and I were driving to a beautiful English country wedding. We dutifully typed the address into Google Maps and set off on our merry way. As we drove, we found ourselves on increasingly smaller roads, with less and less tarmac, and an impending sense that Google might not have been as trustworthy as first thought to lead us on the best route to our destination.

The Israelites may have had similar thoughts regarding God's questionable route selection for their journey to the Promised Land. Unlike Google, however, God had a didactic purpose in taking them the long way home: protection and education.

The most direct way to their destination would have been the Via Maris route. As a popular well travelled trade route between Egypt and Asia, it had good, easy roads with the opportunity to buy food and water along the way. From Succoth, the whole journey would have been approximately 150 miles of comfortable walking to reach Gaza.

What the Israelites didn't realise, though, is that this shorter route would have led them through "Philistine country" (Exodus 18:17). There would have been danger of conflict and warfare with tribes along the way, not to mention encountering the Egyptian forts that manned the main roads. In leading them on a longer, less comfortable route, God was protecting them from unforeseen danger. Leaving directly from lives of slavery, they were not 'battle ready' as some translations imply, but were undisciplined, unprepared, and untrained to face foes. As such, at the first sight of conflict there was the potential they "might change their minds and return to Egypt" (v.17).

God knew the Israelites were fickle. There were many moments to come where they even felt nostalgia for their previous life in

Egypt (Exodus 14:11-12, Numbers 14:1-4). "Change their minds" in this passage comes from the Hebrew word *nacham* which means 'to be sorry', or to 'console oneself'. Yet the Israelites aren't alone in leading with their emotions and seeking the comfortable way. We all desire an easy route and are tempted to change our minds when things don't appear straightforward or turn out as we expect. In our hearts we may plan the future and map out our course "but the Lord establishes [our] steps" (Proverbs 16:9).

Leading the Israelites on a longer, more uncomfortable route also meant the Lord could grow their faith and educate them in what it looked like to trust Him in strange places and unknown timings. When you trust Google maps, you are relying on the information it is feeding you to get you to your destination. But the Lord is not an algorithm or a selection of cleverly crafted technology. He is the omnipotent, omniscient, and omnipresent God who sees the end of our journey as well as where we find ourselves today.

He displayed His presence, guidance, and provision to the Israelites through the theophany of the pillars of cloud and fire: A visible, moving, leading manifestation of God. How comforting for the Israelites to see the presence of God with them twenty-four seven! The express mention of "day or night" (v.22) encompasses the ever-present love of God, continually guiding and protecting His people.

We may not have clouds today, but God has not left us without a guide and light. The Word of God is both a "lamp for our feet" and a light for our path (Psalm 119:105)—effective and powerful (Isaiah 55:11). Be reassured that no matter how long your journey, no matter how uncomfortable it feels, God has not changed. He will lead you on the very path you need to reach your destination safely and with greater faith and intimacy in Him.

Thank God for the ways in which He is leading you regardless of whether you understand them. Are there any areas of your life that you need to recommit to His care where you have tried to take the reins and go your own way?

DAY FOURTEEN

Hold Your Peace

JENNA MARIE MASTERS

Exodus 14

A few years ago, it appeared my husband was being offered a job out of state. The company flew us to North Carolina, set us up with a real estate agent, and promised my husband that a job offer would be coming the following week. We were nervous but excited, and had started to dream of a new adventure. We felt God was in front of us the whole way, leading and preparing our hearts for this, and we were ready.

But the offer never came.

All the dreaming and preparing came to a halt, and we didn't see God in front of us leading the way anymore. All we could see were crumbling hopes. I think of how the Israelites must have felt when suddenly their view of the front of the caravan changed from the leading presence of the angel of the Lord to a wall of water, blocking their way to freedom.

Moses tells the people, "the Lord will fight for you; you need only to be still" (v.14). But in the next moment, God says, "Move." It appears Moses and God are giving contradicting instructions, but the phrase "you need only to be still" is not necessarily a physical command. The King James Version reads, "The Lord shall fight for you, and ye shall hold your peace" (Exodus 14:14). Here Moses is encouraging the Israelites to quietly trust God as He urges them to move forward in faith, into the unknown.

They are now left with a choice, just as we often are: *Will they complain about their circumstances changing or choose to trust God's promises, even when they can't 'see' Him in front of them?*

Moses does the latter.

Moses trusted when God moved, and for a good reason. He chose

49

to fix his eyes not on what was seen but on what was *unseen* (2 Corinthians 4:18). God had promised Moses that He would bring them up out of the misery they suffered in Egypt (Exodus 3:17), and he believed Him.

Sometimes we confuse God's *moving* for *leaving*. God promises never to leave us nor forsake us. He didn't leave the Israelitess, He simply moved from the front of the caravan to the back. *Why?* Pharaoh's army was coming from behind!

In this stunning record of history, the angel of God enters as a pillar of cloud by day and fire by night to lead the Israelites out of Egypt. So when the angel of the Lord moved, the pillar moved with Him. Now, with the cloud gone, they could see the waves clearly. This must have been frightening.

But consider this: *If they couldn't see the obstacle in their way, how could they experience their Way-maker?* In other words: no waves, no wonder. Witnessing the sea part before them, they walked between walls of water towards their promised freedom.

What do we do when it appears God has withdrawn from the front of our battle? Do we trust that He moves for good reasons, that He plans to prosper us, not to harm us? Could it be He moves because something is coming from behind? Like Pharaoh's army, or, in our case, a company takeover?

Three months after our dreams of moving were struck down, we found out that the man who took the job we had prayed for lost his position under new management. We would've moved across the country, away from our family and community, invested in a new home, only to be jobless within months. Wow.

God didn't leave us. We believe He was fighting on our behalf for my husband *not* to get the job offer. He saw what was coming from behind, rushed into the spaces we couldn't see, and protected us. If you don't feel God is in front of your battle anymore, then maybe He's behind you, taking care of business. Or perhaps He's moved so you have a better view of the miracle that is on its way. We may not always know how God is moving, but we can hold our peace as He directs our path.

What are the barriers or 'walls of water' you're facing in your life? Take some time to ask the Lord to know what it looks like to "hold your peace" in this season, and then thank Him that He is with you, even now.

He Cares for You

PAULA MORRISON

Exodus 15

Life circumstances can change in a moment, *can't they?* One day you can be celebrating, and the next day trouble can knock on your door causing the situation to alter very quickly.

I think back to when I was pregnant with my first child. It had been a joyous surprise and an easy pregnancy until a routine appointment during my lunch break led to a sudden hospital admission and the birth of a very small premature baby. I never did return to my work desk, and in those early days, weeks, and months, I continued to ask my heavenly Father the question, *"Will You care for me?"*—not because I didn't believe God was loving, caring, and could provide for my needs but, rather, I needed the assurance He would do it for *me!*

In this chapter, we see the joy of the Israelites as they celebrate a defining event in the Old Testament: the Crossing of the Red Sea. It is a moment in history that the people of Israel will forever remember, and we see an example of this in Psalm 77:19-20 where hundreds of years later they are still singing about their deliverance from Egypt.

We can only imagine the beautiful scene as Miriam and the other women are dancing with tambourines and singing to the Lord, the great Deliverer of the newborn nation of Israel, who has just triumphed gloriously over the entire army of Pharaoh. At the heart of the song of Moses and Miriam, is the question: "Who among the gods is like you, Lord? Who is like you—majestic in holiness, awesome in glory, working wonders?" (v.11). The answer is a resounding "no one," of course, because there are no other gods before the one true God Almighty.

It is interesting that immediately after coming through the waters, the Lord leads His people into the wilderness, and we read in the remaining verses of this chapter, a story of bitter water made sweet. *Marah* is the Hebrew word for 'bitter' and it refers to stagnant water as opposed to fresh spring water. The miracle we are seeing here then is God not only providing water for the Israelites to drink but also bringing life from that which was dead.

The wilderness turns out to be a place of testing, because even after their miraculous deliverance from the plagues in Egypt, the Passover, and their journey through the Red Sea, the question they are really asking is, *"Will God care for us?"* Like children they are grumbling about their current needs but their underlying concern is whether God can be trusted or if He will treat them like He treated the Egyptians. God assures them, however, that if they listen and obey His instructions, He will provide living water for them because, "I am the Lord, who heals you" (v.26). The safest place for the Israelites to be at this time was in the presence of the Lord, listening to Him and following His commands. And the same is true for us, too.

I love the fact that just beyond the place of testing, when they are wondering if God would indeed come through for them, they come to Elim—an oasis in the desert with twelve springs and seventy palm trees. Here God provides them with the living water He promised He would, one spring for each of the tribes of Israel and seventy palm trees representing the number of Jacob's household that first went into Egypt. By this action, God proved that He could not only be trusted to care for them, but also that His provision was one of abundance and perfection.

The same is true for us. Let's remember that, in the midst of bitter hard seasons as we do our best to listen to and obey the Lord, we can trust in His care for us. And just beyond our view there may be a sweet season of blessing beyond our wildest imagining.

Where are you struggling to believe that God will care for you? Honestly share with Him the places where you feel forgotten and hopeless and invite Holy Spirit to strengthen you to keep walking in trusting obedience. Thank Him in advance for the provision He has prepared for you.

A Foundation of Trust

AMBER PALMER

Exodus 16

Forty-five days have passed since the Israelites' feet have touched Egyptian ground. Although it's safe to say they have been through a lot, despite all the miraculous wonders they've experienced along the way, it doesn't take long for them to develop a negative cycle of grumbling and complaining about their new living conditions. The life they thought they left Egypt for doesn't quite match their high expectations, and as hunger sets in, Exodus 16 not only depicts more grumbling but also records them actually crying out for their life back in Egypt. You know, the life of slavery they originally begged God to save them from. It is amazing how discomfort can skew our reality and lead us away from trusting our heavenly Father.

I have been guilty of reading about the Israelites through a judgemental lens, hyper-focused on where they fall short in their journey through the wilderness. But this time around, my heart was keenly aware of how God graciously provides for their needs each time the Israelites grumble and cry about their circumstances. By putting into place a promising cycle of hearing their cries and responding, He demonstrates His glory and builds on their foundation of trust by affirming He is their ultimate provider, not only for this journey but for *everything*. In verse 23, God adds another element to this relationship of provision when He commands the Israelites to observe a day of rest, which will later be known as the Sabbath. He hasn't given the Ten Commandments to the Israelites just yet, but we already know rest is important to God because in Genesis 2:2-3, He made a point to rest, bless, and sanctify the seventh day after creation.

What does this type of rest look like for the Israelites? On the sixth day of the week, they are permitted to gather a double portion of their allotted manna and quail to hold them over through the Sabbath with the promise that the leftovers would not be spoiled. This act gives them further opportunity to trust God as their provider and practice being obedient in what He asks of them. In this way, God lovingly leads His people to personally know Him as Jehovah Jireh, 'the Lord will provide', finding true rest in His promise of provision.

Observing the Sabbath not only gives our bodies a break from the 'doing', but allows space to make sure our hearts are in a posture of rest. A heart at rest is a heart wholly devoted to God. It's a heart that with humility and gratitude, surrenders control over to Him. And through this posture of rest we find a deeper relationship with God. There is connection and faith building in the letting go, and an unbreakable foundation being built in our surrender and ability to have peace in God's provisions, even when it differs from our humanly-crafted expectations.

Similar to the Israelites' experience, we each have our own wilderness journey towards our own Promised Land of eternity with the Lord. As we run the race set before us, we can find peace knowing God hears our cries and is faithful in filling our needs with His provisions. Our cup runneth over with the promise that Jesus Himself is our Sabbath-rest (Hebrews 4:9), and we no longer have to work in our own strength, striving or using special tactics to try to make ourselves right with God. Until our journey back to His presence is finished, may faith, trust, and obedience be our rested responses to God's blessings in our lives.

Take stock of your own heart. How would you describe its current posture? What practical steps and rhythms might you need to put in place to enter into His rest?

DAY SEVENTEEN

Steady Till Sunset

JENNA MARIE MASTERS

Exodus 17

Want to know a secret? On court dates for our foster daughter, I'd ask God to send His mightiest angels to fight in court on her behalf. I was so bold I even requested Michael the archangel. *Why not be specific and ask for the best?* Surely, our children are worth it!

I believe with all my heart that God honoured that prayer. So when the most critical court date of all loomed before us, although I was shaking and nauseous, I knew God had an army ready to storm the courtroom. And I was on my knees, prepared to battle with the best of them.

I remember my forehead pressed to the cold tile floor, gulping down sobs as whispered prayers rattled my lips,

Jesus, press Your wisdom on the heart of the judge.
Angels, use your swords to strike down every lie.
Father God, fight for my daughter's life; You promise to give her hope and a future.

Little did I anticipate that even in my passion and fervour, halfway through the court hearing I'd grow exhausted—emotionally, spiritually, and physically. Just like Moses, I grew weary.

We read in this passage that every time Moses' exhausted arms drop, His people begin to lose the battle against the Amalekites (v.11). It's the same for all of us; when we try to keep our arms raised during our battles without the help of our brothers and sisters in Christ, there are consequences.

When Aaron and Hur see their friend struggling, they set a stone beneath him so he can rest and hold his arms steady until sunset. Together, they are victorious against the enemy. Even before Jesus entered the earthly scene of their lives, they fulfilled the law of

Christ and compassionately and courageously carried each other's burdens (Galatians 6:2). Moses could have swatted the hands of his friends away and refused to sit on the stone. Instead, he modelled that fighting well often looks like allowing others to hold us up and relying on the body of Christ to glorify Him together.

My loving Father wanted me to learn this truth on the kitchen floor that day. I knew that my daughter needed me, but I was a shaking, sweaty, huddled mess with a goldfish cracker crunched under my knee. My strength was gone. And God knew it.

But I'll never forget His Spirit pressing on me. *You have fought well, daughter. Now rest. Let the prayers of others hold you up.* Then God led me away from the thick of the battle to give me a clear view of what was going on. He showed me that hundreds of people were praying for our foster daughter at that *exact* moment. My phone was blowing up with texts; precious people in my life were going to war for her life simultaneously.

Just like that, I was scooped up in peace, knowing that the people who love our family were carrying us to victory. Their love was placed like stones under me, their prayers were holding up my arms, and their faithfulness was keeping me steady till sunset. Now, we rejoice that our foster daughter is now our legal daughter through adoption. But looking back on our journey, I see that just like Moses couldn't have completed the mission God assigned him without leaning on Aaron and Hur, we couldn't have completed ours without our faithful community of believers.

I wonder: *How many 'Amalekites' do we allow to defeat us because we don't surround ourselves with other believers who are ready to go to the top of the hill with us? How many holy callings do we forfeit because we're too prideful to accept the help of others?*

Life will continually threaten to shake God's promises, but we, like Moses, must battle for His Kingdom and purposes and prepare to stand firm until the setting of the sun. But we can't do it alone. "*So speak encouraging words to one another. Build up hope so you'll all be together in this, no one left out, no one left behind. I know you're already doing this; just keep on doing it*" (1 Thessalonians 5:11 MSG).

Ask Holy Spirit to impress on your heart who you need to encourage and lift up in prayer today. Reach out to that person to affirm them and let them know that they're not alone in their battle.

DAY EIGHTEEN
Lighten the load
EMILY TYLER

Exodus 18

We emigrated from the UK to New Zealand with three young children who'd never been on an aeroplane before let alone travelled the longest journey possible on one. Standing in queues to get through customs and passport control, ensuring everyone stayed together and no one was left behind, and dealing with whiny moments of frustration and exhaustion was hard work. I don't know how I would have coped without my husband to 'divide and conquer' and share the burden together. It was a journey we were glad to be making, but it wasn't without its difficulties.

In this chapter we witness Moses share with his father-in-law Jethro his own challenging journey and "all the hardships they had met along the way" (Exodus 18:8). The Hebrew for 'hardships' is *telaah* and encapsulates the idea of being weary, referring to something that makes one exhausted either physically or emotionally. The Septuagint translates this as *mochthos*: hard and difficult labour involving suffering and implying an unusual exertion of energy and effort. In other words, this was no small journey of deliverance.

It is with fresh eyes then that Jethro observes the queues Moses faced as arbitrator "for the people" (v.14) and questions why he is attempting to stand and carry the burden alone. There would have been at least 600,000 men in the camp at this point (Exodus 12:37), yet it appears Moses hasn't considered asking anyone to help. Nor has it occurred to any of the men to offer to share the load. There's a danger when faced with overwhelming tasks that we become culture-bound doing things a particular way because *that's how it's always been done*. Sometimes it takes an outside perspective to highlight the unnecessary pressure we're putting ourselves under.

On our travels, our barely three-year-old child wanted to lift suitcases off the conveyor belt. Our response was much the same as Jethro's comment to Moses: "The work is too heavy for you; you cannot handle it alone" (v.18). The word for 'heavy' here is *kabed*. This is the same word used in Exodus 17:12 where Moses was unable to keep his arms in the air during the Amalekite battle. Moses would have been reminded of his need for Aaron and Hur to come alongside him and share the burden. In the same way, Jethro points out that Moses needs assistance from others to make his "load lighter" (v.23). The word for 'load' here, *qalal*, was also used in Jonah 1:5 when sailors were throwing cargo overboard to prevent the ship from sinking.

Jethro lovingly watches his son-in-law and recognises that if he tries to continue without help then he'll likely keep sinking and go under. All too often, my own toddler-like "me do it" independence and desire to be all things for all people results in a burden that is too heavy to handle. But God's children were never meant to carry heaviness alone. Paul calls us to "share each other's burdens" (Galatians 6:2 NLT) and, in doing so, fulfil Jesus' law of love.

Moses' task is an important one that must be administered with godliness and wisdom. Jethro wisely gives Moses a four-step plan for lightening his load. First, continue with what God has called you to (v.19), then if faced with a load too great to bear, go to God in prayer (v.19). Thirdly, Moses was to teach the people and "show them the way they are to live and how they are to behave" (v.20). Finally, he was to *chazah* the ones who would help. *Chazah* means to select and choose wisely, to gaze at and mentally perceive (after taking time for reflection). These men were to be God-fearing, able, and those who held fast to truth (v.21). It matters who we yoke ourselves with. It matters where we go for help.

We have the ultimate burden-bearer in Jesus. He lovingly calls us to stop struggling on our own, and instead come to Him, because He promises not to "lay anything heavy or ill-fitting" on us (Matthew 11:30 MSG). Go to Him for help today.

What is it that you're trying to carry alone that is too heavy? Surrender it back to Jesus and invite Him to show you what steps you need to take to lighten the load.

_____
_____
_____
_____
_____
_____
_____
_____
_____
_____
_____
_____
_____
_____
_____
_____
_____
_____
_____
_____
_____
_____

DAY NINETEEN

Invited Near

ASHLEY KELLY

Exodus 19

I am a rule-follower by nature. If there is a sign posted, I will obey whatever it says. If there is a boundary drawn, I will stay far from it. And if anyone doesn't follow the rules, I will be inwardly very annoyed—though outwardly I'll often pretend to be more easy going than I actually am. For the most part, I believe rules and restrictions are put into place with the best intentions—for protection and safety. Maybe that's an optimistic 'the-cup-is-half-full' way of thinking, and I'm sure it's also influenced by the culture of freedom in which I am fortunate to live. But rules, I believe, are there for a purpose.

In this passage, God instructs Moses to put some literal boundaries in place as He prepares to "come down on Mount Sinai in the sight of all the people" (v.11). Here, the restrictions keeping the people from coming close or touching the mountain—the place where God's presence will descend—are set to protect the people. God even directs them to spend days preparing themselves for His presence. More rules. More *things to do*. All for the purpose of keeping the people safe, whether they understand that or not. Their understanding holds no bearing on the necessity of the rules.

The presence of God is holy and perfect. The people are not. The instruction to "be ready by the third day" (v.11) is one of preparation. They are to consecrate themselves and keep themselves pure in preparation to witness the holy presence of the Lord. Their sin, their 'uncleanness', actually cannot exist near their holy and perfect God. If they ignore the boundaries and approach the mountain, death would be the inevitable result. So, these limits drawn by God and implemented by Moses are for the good of the people.

God is going to come close to His people on the third day. This is what they are about to experience. Yet, even though *He* is going to draw near, *they* cannot. They must follow the rules. In a sense, God is still unapproachable. So close, yet so far.

Thousands of years later, there is another *third day*, but this time the boundaries are removed. Torn. No longer needed. All thanks to Jesus. This time as He comes near, the people are invited to also come near. When the resurrected Jesus approaches His disciples, they are unsure and troubled, to which He says: "See my hands and my feet, that it is I myself. Touch me, and see" (Luke 24:39 ESV). *Touch Me. Come close to Me. Approach Me.*

Through Jesus and His blood spilled on the cross, we also are invited near. We also are given access to our mighty, powerful, holy, and perfect God. What once was unapproachable and unattainable is now available to us. Those boundaries of old have been removed, no longer keeping us at a distance from our Creator. We can now have "confidence to enter the holy places by the blood of Jesus, by the new and living way that he opened for us through the curtain," which means we can and should "draw near with a true heart in full assurance of faith" (Hebrews 10:19-22 ESV).

Unlike the Israelites, we can run up that mountain with abandon, freely and with confidence. We can boldly approach the throne, the very presence of God, trusting that Jesus has already paved the way. Yet this nearness—living in close relationship with our God and He with us—is merely a sneak peek of what is to come. Revelation 21 and 22 reveal a time everlasting in which He will be forever near to us just as we will forever be near to Him. No boundaries. Nothing holding us back. Oh what a glorious day that will be!

Have you inadvertently distanced yourself from Jesus? What does it look like to intentionally draw near and come into His presence again today? What do you sense Him saying to you as you draw close?

DAY TWENTY

The Redeemed Life

MAZHAR KEFALI

Exodus 20

The people of Israel entered Egypt as a family and exited as a nation. In the previous chapter, Yahweh has established and defined the nature of His relationship with Israel. From all the nations of the earth, He has chosen this one nation to be His representatives and witness to the watching world—"a kingdom of priests and a holy nation" (Exodus 19:5-6). They are His sovereign choice, intended to live in such a way as to reveal His nature, so that the surrounding nations would say, in effect, "so *this* is what Yahweh is like."

This new nation required clear guidelines and 'laws' in how to live and conduct themselves amongst all the other nations and cultures in a way that represented Yahweh and His purposes on the earth. In this chapter, we are given a sense of these laws in concise form, commonly known as 'The Ten Commandments'. They are also known as the 'Decalogue' which literally means 'ten words'. This a more accurate title as this is how they are spoken of in the Old Testament (Exodus 34:28; Deuteronomy 4:13; 10:4). The Hebrew word for *commandments* literally means 'something spoken, words'. These are living, breathing words, from the very mouth of Yahweh (v.1).

It has become a tragedy that they have since been seen as 'rules' instead of what they truly are—a revelation of the nature of God that then translates into living in a way that is consistent with His nature and attributes. These words from Yahweh Himself explain why and how God's people are to express wholehearted devotion, love, and loyalty to Him, and reflect His heart towards others who are created in His image by showing them honour, respect, love, and mercy.

The people of Israel were so overwhelmed by the manifestation of God's holiness in this revelation of His code of conduct that they did not want to get close to Him. They feared, in their sinfulness, that they would die in the presence of Yahweh, and they wanted Moses to represent them in terms of their relationship with God (vv.18-19). There is, in a sense, a sadness in this request as the Father desires that His children have an intimate personal relationship with Him instead of one that is derived second-hand through an intermediary. While this was the way of things in the Old Testament, God opened the way for a direct personal relationship with Himself with no other mediator required except "the man Christ Jesus" (1 Timothy 2:5-6).

Moses encourages the people, despite their fear, that this manifestation of God is for their own good, instilling in them a healthy and holy fear of Yahweh that would act as a strong deterrent to sinning against Him (v.20). The Lord then reveals and reinstates that He desires single-hearted devotion and loyalty from His people, expressed in sacrificial worship (vv.22-24a). Verse 24b reveals to the people what the Ten Commandments are essentially about—the honour of Yahweh and His name. The resulting consequence of His name being honoured is that He will bring about blessing to His people.

Philosopher and poet Heinrich Heine said, "Show me your redeemed life and I might be inclined to believe in your Redeemer." The Father desires for His children to reflect the family identity and the kingdom culture through their wholehearted love and loyalty to Him, and treat others in such a way that reflects Him. For if we do, the watching world might say, "so that is what God is like," and hopefully, one day, even be drawn into His family themselves.

Spend some time meditating on the Ten Commandments. How do you sense Holy Spirit convicting and inviting you to align with God's character and ways through these laws? Ask Him to empower you to reflect the Father and His Kingdom well.

DAY TWENTY-ONE
Revolt Against Revenge
EMILY TYLER

Exodus 21

When someone wrongs me, I confess that the first thoughts in my head are not always benevolent, generous, and forgiving. More likely, if someone hurts or mistreats me in some way, my instinctive reaction is to 'get even', make them 'pay', or administer justice (as *I* see fit).

I suspect that many of the Israelites who had been attacked, beaten, or harmed in some way might have felt a similar desire for retaliation and revenge. Acutely aware of this very human condition in the hearts of His children, God created a code of law for the Israelites to live by that would ensure justice in their day-to-day disputes. Their governance was theocratic in nature; it all came from God which meant there was no danger that human selfishness or sin would dictate the laws of the land and people.

The truth is, we all relate to the natural instinct of the "eye for eye" transaction in verse 24: *You hurt me, so now I get to hurt you back.* But this revenge mentality was not what God was aiming for when He implemented these laws. In fact, when you look at the cultures surrounding the Israelites and the behaviours that were accepted in their day, these laws were more about instilling protection, security, and faith: Faith that *God* was the One who would administer justice, so the Israelites didn't have to.

It's no surprise the topic of slavery comes right at the beginning of the law because the Israelites—a habitually enslaved people—needed a new model from which to work. In spite of their new-found freedom from the Egyptians, God needed to instill a new understanding of what it meant to 'own' a slave and have someone work for you. He needed to ensure they unlearnt their warped Egyptian experiences. (As an aside, oftentimes I wonder if much of what God wants to teach me stems from 'unlearning' things I have absorbed from the culture I find myself living in).

70

The pagan nations surrounding the Israelites did not treat slaves as human and granted them no rights. The idea that a master should receive some sort of punishment for mistreatment of a slave was unheard of. As difficult as it might be to understand from our perspective in history, these laws provided value and significance to slaves as men made in the image of God, the emphasis being to create safe limitations and boundaries in relation to how they should be treated. Spurgeon notes that these laws were made to repress slavery, to confine it within very narrow bounds and, ultimately, to put an end to it. The reality was, since the role of slave or servant was established by God as being more like a contractor with employee rights, many wanted to remain working for and serving their owners beyond their six-year 'out' period because it was actually good and beneficial for them to remain.

When we look to Jesus' understanding of the whole law, we see it hung on these two commandments: loving God and loving people (Matthew 22:37-40). So, if we're reading this chapter through the lens of love, we start to see that the law God created was all about enabling His people to love Him and to love each other.

Our culture continues the natural desire of looking for someone to pay, but it's time to revolt against revenge, unlearn its ways, and instead follow the model of love that Jesus laid down for us. He taught us that it's not about, "eye for eye, and tooth for tooth" but turning the other cheek, giving more than is asked of us, and going beyond what we're forced to do (Matthew 5:38-42). We have a new model to work from because the law was fulfilled in Christ (Matthew 5:17). And just as the original rules set out to ensure love was at the centre, our law also has its foundation in love. So the next time you're tempted to make someone else 'pay', remember Jesus already paid the price in full on their behalf—and on yours, too.

Where do you need to trust God for justice? Surrender that situation to Him and invite Holy Spirit to empower you to forgive those who have wronged you. Release them from your judgment by name and allow Holy Spirit to minister healing to your heart.

Boundaries of Faithfulness

SHELLEY JOHNSON

Exodus 22

I watched as a high school friend flew off to college like a caged bird set free. No longer under the rule of her tyrannical father who had dictated her every move, she resolved to say yes to everything. Never having had the opportunity to practice self-governance, my friend underestimated the need for self-control and some well-placed boundaries. Eventually, this little chick found herself in a different kind of cage—one created from her own excessive choices.

Perhaps it helps us as we read through another chapter packed full of laws to see the Hebrew people through a similar lens. Like my unrestrained friend, these former slaves had been controlled by a restrictive authority. For generations, they'd never had to govern themselves. Someone else had always overseen them.

But now, at the foot of Mount Sinai, this community is able, for the first time, to exert their own will as they experience freedom and all of its follies. Without taskmasters to dole out the punishments for wrongdoings, God's people respond as emotions dictate. A stolen goat elicits rage that leads to revenge. A burned field evokes yearnings for vengeance. Unchecked, the Hebrew people are killing each other over common crimes.

That's when their divine Sovereign steps-in to offer a better way to navigate life in community. Civil laws, such as the ones we read today, offer a restrained path for justice that works like compensation rather than carnage. God's approach offers His people a way to make things right when they do something wrong. God's system institutes restitution to curb the tendency for revenge.

The Hebrew word for restitution, *shalem*, means 'to be in covenant peace'. Its prolific use in this chapter—upwards of fifteen times—implies its importance. God wants His covenant people to employ this practice as a means of restoring and keeping social order. He desires them to *shalem* in order to keep the *shalom*—a peace of completeness, soundness, and welfare. In His loving kindness, God seeks the best for His people, so His laws are less like cages to contain His children and more like rules to help them remain faithful to their life as His chosen people.

As we read through another chapter of law, may we relent in our eye-rolling towards these children of God who have no boundaries and tend towards bloodshed. May we recognise God's efforts to establish a nation in which justice is enforced more equitably and where the powerless are protected. May we have grace for them just as Jesus has for us.

Much like our wilderness-wandering ancestors, we are apt to overreact when wronged and take advantage of those who are weak. In an era when anger at injustice bubbles just beneath the surface while hatred spews in all directions, we too easily fail to self-govern with peace in mind.

Jesus may not have given us hundreds of laws to follow in order to be His 'holy people' (v.31), but He does have expectations for obedience because He knows our tendency for self-focus. He knows that if we are to live well as His witnesses in the world, we must be able to abide by His commands to love God and to love others as ourselves (Matthew 22:36-40).

To love God is to obey Him (1 John 2:5) and to delight in His Word (1 John 5:3). To love others is to extend the grace we've been given and to offer the peace of Christ in all our actions and reactions (1 Peter 4:8-10). And as we determine to live within the boundaries of such faithfulness, may we—like the Israelites—discover the joy and peace of God's holy presence.

Where in your life do you have an absence of boundaries? Sit with Holy Spirit and invite Him to show you what 'boundaries of faithfulness' you need to put in place at this time so you can walk in shalom—in the peace and wholeness God intended you to.

_____

_____

_____

_____

_____

_____

_____

_____

_____

_____

_____

_____

_____

_____

_____

_____

_____

_____

_____

_____

_____

_____

_____

_____

Keeping in Step with Heaven

JEFF MCKEE

Exodus 23

The provision of a dedicated angel to help take the Promised Land was an incredible gift to the people of Israel. Yet this new relationship would take some care. Moses makes it clear—despite the many advantages of having this angel among them—they could expect him to be a very exacting companion (vv.20-21).

This angel bore God's name (v.21)—the One who judges righteousness and wickedness, drives out entire people groups from their own, and allocates inheritances afresh. To dwell in favour, His people would need to walk in the fear of the Lord. The Israelites would need to be different to those they dispossessed in order to honour that sacred name and keep the angel on side. They could not pervert justice for personal gain, and it would be best if they lent a hand whenever they saw need (vv.4-9). In fact, they ought to become champions of justice. Even the cadence of their lives should benefit the needy and honour the Lord. Routine testing of what was in their hands—land, servants, and animals—was intended to embed margin and allow for habitual giving back to those worse off. They were also advised to pause in their desire to prosper for another reason—to worship together and offer something back to God.

Following Moses' advice proved difficult. The angel favoured them and brought them victory whenever he could, yet there were also plenty of times when he administered judgement on them, as Moses had warned.

Years down the track, the same angel oversaw the victories of David and the glory of Israel under Solomon. He was intimately involved through the troubled days of the judges, administering discipline whenever they strayed. The prophet Samuel describes a scene where this angel literally culls the numbers of the people of God, that is until the Lord stayed his hand just before he laid waste to Jerusalem (2 Samuel 24:16).

Eventually the people become completely corrupt. Having neglected all the words of Moses, the angel stands aside to allow them to be carried off into exile by the Babylonians. However, somewhere along the line he bonded once more with this on-again, off-again nation called Israel. Now he is known, not as 'my angel' as God first introduced him, but as their prince (Daniel 10:21). At this point, we even learn his name—Michael (Daniel 10:13,21; 12:1). The exacting angel of the Lord had, over the centuries, become a personal companion of God's people—one who had remained devoted to watching over them and serving them, even when they had done their dash and lost their land. Finally, when it appears that all is over for them, Michael fights for the answer to a prayer to get through (Daniel 9:2-3; 10:21), one that would bring an end to their exile and restore their fortunes.

The story of Michael and Israel, his charge, teaches us much about the benefits of walking in righteousness, not least, that we ought to keep the angels responsible for our care favourable toward us. After all, they don't miss a thing!

But there is something more for us to understand. In Christ, God has elevated us, His people, above Michael and his kin (Ephesians 2:6, Hebrews 1:14). He has put His name on us (John 14-16)—now *we* are the ones who share His name! Through His Holy Spirit we have become like an angel of God to the people all around us. Like Michael the archangel, our role may often both delight and frustrate us, depending on the responsiveness and condition of heart of those we stand with. Perhaps it might be best if, like Michael, we allow them to get under our skin, so we become their champions rather than their judges, because our attitude may be as significant as theirs to the outcome of the mission!

How is God inviting you to keep in step with Heaven and become a 'champion of justice' at this time?

_____

_____

_____

_____

_____

_____

_____

_____

_____

_____

_____

_____

_____

_____

_____

_____

_____

_____

_____

_____

_____

_____

His Whole Self

KAY GLEAVES

Exodus 24

If you haven't already studied this chapter in Exodus, I encourage you to go back and read it first, paying particular attention to verse 8. Depending on the version you're reading, it's going to say that Moses "sprinkled" or "splashed" or "threw" blood on the people.

Woah. No thank you with the sheep or goat blood! Please don't splash that on or near me! *I'm glad we are covered by the blood of Jesus, aren't you?*

This covering of blood mentioned in verse 8 is a foreshadowing of how Jesus' blood would one day cover *us*. It was also used symbolically to show that the children of Israel were tied to the covenant—covered so they could stay connected.

God is so kind. He is so loving. Because He desired greater connection with us, He created a way that meant we didn't have to continue to be splashed with the blood of a dead animal. He made a better way—and not just a way, but a new covenant. I like to explain a covenant as a two-way promise to stay in relationship with one another. God covered us with the blood of His Son, so He could stay connected to us. I know God is not going to break His end of the covenant, and His loving kindness makes me want to stay connected to Him and not break mine.

As I stopped and pondered all of this, I felt the prompting of Holy Spirit to go back to the top of the chapter and read through it again. *If God is so kind and so loving, what else does it reveal about His character and attributes?*

Let me just highlight some of what I found:

God is present, available, and inclusive (v.1).

God is holy, clear, and precise (v.2).

God is an author, and He hasn't quit speaking today (v.3).

God desires for us to know His Word, and He wants our worship (vv.4-6).

God is redeemer, covenant-maker, and promise-keeper (vv.7-8).

God is approachable (v.9).

God is abundant with riches and cloaked in glory; abounding in grandeur that He wants to show us (v.10).

God is a gentleman—gracious and engaging (v.11).

God is welcoming as He invites and instructs (vv.12-14).

God is patient (vv.15-16).

God is miraculous, magnificent, and full of splendor and awe that He wants to lavish upon us (v.17).

God lingers. He takes His time with us and longs to remain with us (v.18).

I wonder if you need to hear today that God is not missing. He is not mad. He is not quiet, nor is He reserved. He is a gracious gentleman; and while He instructs, He also leans in close to be engaging, inviting, and lingering. He desires to lavish us with Himself, His abundance, and His time. He holds nothing back. He doesn't keep Himself hidden from us and there is so much more He longs to reveal if only we take time to sit and see, to wonder and ask.

Oh, friend, I hope you see Him. I hope you catch a glimpse of the wholeness, fullness, and audaciousness of our God who not only made a way, but also, who brought His whole self to us, not just because He loves us, but because He longs for us. He longs for *you*. *Does your heart need to be reminded of who God is today?* Ask Him to reveal Himself to you—He will.

Make your own list of God's attributes from this chapter. Spend some time meditating on the wonder of who He is and give thanks that He has made a way for you to be connected to Him forever.

_____

_____

_____

_____

_____

_____

_____

_____

_____

_____

_____

_____

_____

_____

_____

_____

_____

_____

_____

_____

_____

_____

_____

_____

_____

_____

DAY TWENTY-FIVE

From the Heart

AMBER PALMER

Exodus 25

I find it quite the challenge to cook healthy meals for my family—honestly, life feels busy enough and any attempt to incorporate clean meal plans and prep time into my day leaves me completely frazzled. To add another layer of difficulty, I dislike cooking and my eyes glaze over if the recipe list contains more than three ingredients and steps to make it. All too quickly I find myself shutting down and settling for a faster and easier processed dinner option instead.

Reading through all the specific details of the Tabernacle in Exodus 25 can feel similarly overwhelming and tempt me to rush towards the end of the passage, onto the next chapter. But it is important to fight against the urge for quick and easy, because if we don't, we might miss God in the beautiful list of details and glaze over His great purpose to dwell with us. It was His ultimate desire for the Israelites, after all, and is still His heart for us today!

One of the details in this chapter that can be easily overlooked yet holds deep meaning is the powerful opening sentence, "The Lord spoke to Moses" (v.1 NKJV). Moses could have simply given the Israelites, and future readers like us, a bullet-point list or a quick narrative summary of what was spoken between them, but God wanted to make sure His people knew His instructions came from His own voice, highlighting the personal connection He longed for with His people.

Verse 2 contains another important detail I missed until recently. God tells Moses to ask the Israelites to provide the necessary parts for the Tabernacle *if their heart is prompted to do so.* He didn't force them to give up the materials or command them to follow His instructions with an ultimatum attached. Instead He provides a beautiful opportunity for the Israelistes to serve Him with a heart offering, demonstrating faithful obedience, and their own desire to dwell with Him. In response to this special request directly from God, the Israelites feel compelled to provide their Lord with whatever He needs to accomplish the Tabernacle, an action that solidifies their faith and devotion to their God.

Looking at the list of supplies God gives to Moses, the Israelites might have initially wondered where in the middle of the desert all of these precious materials would come from. I have no doubt they had an 'aha God' moment, however, when they remembered Moses telling them to ask the Egyptians for articles of silver and gold, and for clothing, before their exit from Egypt. Way back when the Israelites fled from their lives of slavery, God was already preparing the construction of the Tabernacle. He is a faithful Provider! The Israelites had just what God needed from them.

Jesus Himself is the perfect example of an offering from the heart when He obediently tells God in John 22:42, "yet not my will, but yours be done." Jesus became like the precious materials used in the Tabernacle—a necessary offering for God to dwell with His people once again. He was willing to take on our burdens and be the ultimate sacrifice for our sins.

What a beautiful promise it is knowing that God will provide for us and that He deeply desires a relationship with us. May we easily surrender our hearts to God as an offering, knowing He is faithful in fulfilling His promises, as we rest in the depth of His love for us.

Is there anything God has been asking you to offer up to Him that you have been resisting? What is holding you back? How does meditating on His faithfulness soften your heart to willingly be obedient?

Not a Barrier in Sight

AMBER PALMER

Exodus 26

When my children were little, finding five minutes of sanctuary time alone was usually only possible when I was hiding in the bathroom. As soon as I shut the door behind me, I would hear the pitter patter of tiny feet headed in my direction and sweet voices yelling out for me. They would shimmy their backs up against the door that acted as the barrier between me and them. Even though they couldn't be *with* me, they wanted to be as close to my presence as possible, staying in my vicinity until I was ready to come back out.

Although the bathroom door acted as a barrier between us so I could catch my breath from motherhood for a few minutes, God required a special barrier In order for Him to dwell amongst His people. He needed to ensure there was a way He could protect the unholy from the holy. In order to make this happen, God directs His people to make a *badal. Badal* is the Hebrew word for 'veil' which means 'to separate'. Hanging from gold hooks on four pillars of acacia wood, overlaid with gold, on four bases of silver, the veil, or curtain would "separate the Holy Place from the Most Holy Place" (v.33).

Back in Genesis, God had dwelled with His people without the need for barriers, but once sin was brought into the Garden of Eden after Adam and Eve ate the forbidden fruit, the consequence delivered to them was separation from Him. As we read in Genesis 3:23-24: "Therefore the Lord God sent him out of the garden of Eden. . . He drove out the man, and at the east of the garden He placed the cherubim and a flaming sword that turned every way to guard the way to the tree of life" (ESV). Just like the one God placed in the Garden of Eden to guard the tree of life, God instructed His people to skillfully craft cherubim into the veil to guard the most holiest place in the Tabernacle.

I wonder if the Isralietes felt the weight of their sin as their hands worked feverishly, weaving together the fine blue, purple, and scarlet yarn for the veil that would serve as a barrier to God's presence. But, I also wonder if they felt a weight of gratitude that, despite their sin, God still desired to meet with them. As the Israelites worked on the veil which would keep them separate from God, God was working on the perfect plan that would allow them to be together again. Little did they know the promise they held in their hands— one day the veil in the temple would be torn from top to bottom and the barrier would be required no more. (Matthew 27:5).

So what does all this mean for us? The answer lies in these beautiful verses from Hebrews: "Therefore, brothers, since we have confidence to enter the holy places by the blood of Jesus, by the new and living way that he opened for us through the curtain, that is, through his flesh, and since we have a great priest over the house of the God, let us draw near with a true heart in full assurance of faith, with our hearts sprinkled clean from an evil conscience and our bodies washed with pure water" (vv.19-22 ESV).

The veil hanging suspended between the holy and unholy in the Tabernacle and the Temple, foreshadows Jesus suspended on the wooden cross between death and life. Through His sacrifice, Jesus became our veil, the High Priest who we must now go through in order to enter into God's holy presence. With Christ as the mediator of this new and superior covenant (Hebrews 8:6), we can freely and confidently draw near to God, and He can draw near to us—not a barrier in sight.

What are you feeling the weight of—your sin and brokenness or, the wonder that God desires to meet with you? Pause and allow any heaviness you have been carrying to shift to awe that God has made a way for you to fully and freely enter into His presence.

He leaves The light On

JEFF MCKEE

Exodus 27

Some people have an unusual gift of hospitality. It's as though even the atmosphere in their homes extends a welcome, the physical environment combining effortlessly with their natural gifting to make visitors feel like they belong on a whole other level. Perhaps it's the layout, or the way a home is decorated that enables the values and personality of the owner to shine through, sending a clear message to all who enter: "You matter; you belong within these walls."

This was certainly true of the Tabernacle and its heavenly Owner.

Though He was unseen, how He set up 'home' and entertained visitors was evident. Even the name of the central structure, the Tent of Meeting, conveys the sense that encounter and communion with humanity was God's primary goal in this place.

Much of the Old Testament captures shadows of heavenly realities. As a case in point, the Tabernacle was modelled after an actual place of worship where God meets with His own to commune with them in a place beyond our physical existence and understanding—in Heaven. In the same way, the earthly city of Jerusalem, complete with its Temple, was modelled after the mystical capital, often referred to as Zion. Even the festivals in the Jewish calendar echoed the regular cadence of community gatherings above. The consistent theme is the desire for the majestic Adonai to meet with His people regularly, inviting them into His dwelling place.

When Moses ascended the mountain in Exodus 25, God gave him specific instructions and dimensions so he would know how each element of the Tabernacle was to be constructed and how it should look. Those details were important. Apparently, the closer the shadow of a heavenly object mirrors its reality, the more powerfully and tangibly we experience its essence in the here and now. So, when you looked at your surroundings within the Tabernacle you experienced something of paradise. You saw the shape and texture and colour of heavenly architecture and divine interior design. There is something distinctly hospitable about a place that encourages us to view its Owner the same way.

Think about the progressive invitation into intimacy that this structure heralds, welcoming us in by degrees. On their way to the Tent of Meeting, the worshipper would pass the bronze altar. Having no desire for our guilt to keep us away, God made provision for us to find forgiveness so we can approach Him with confidence. Next was the court where richly-coloured linen walls, rising high above their height, it obscured the outside world so the worshipper could fix their attention solely on their forward progression towards the Tent of Meeting.

The interior of the tent was divided by a veil. A whole lot of care went into what was built and placed within the sacred space on the far side of the veil. The furnishings—the Ark of the Covenant with its gold plating, covering statues of cherubim, and mercy seat— provided a drawing power for the presence of God. It was a replica of the very centre of Heaven, an artistic expression of the throne room of God Almighty.

The space on the near side of the veil was not for the Lord; it was a place for people to meet with Him. Their surroundings were intended to elevate their worship, so they could authentically experience an encounter with God who was close at hand. Here a lamp was set that was never allowed to go out. God was literally leaving the light on so that, day or night, whoever entered felt welcome. It seems there was no end to the amount of care and consideration He was prepared to put in so that His people could meet with Him, even though they existed in an entirely different realm.

Today, that lamp still burns in His heavenly home. It always beckoned the people of God, but now it welcomes us to enter deeper still. That lamp lights the way through the torn veil. Let us walk together, beyond physical foreshadowings, into the actual light of His presence.

How are you making your life beautiful and welcoming God into it? Are there any areas where you need to intentionally make space for Him to be with you?

_____

_____

_____

_____

_____

_____

_____

_____

_____

_____

_____

_____

_____

_____

_____

_____

_____

_____

_____

_____

Who Are You Wearing?
ADÉLE DEYSEL

Exodus 28

Jessica Alba as the face of Revlon, Jane Fonda forever aging perfectly with Loréal, and Michael Jordan playing basketball in his Nikes—some people will forever be remembered for their connection with specific brands. Yet, though a contracted sponsorship is generally a mutually beneficial relationship where each endorses the other and the success of the one directly influences both, these 'celebrities' tend to be known not always by their name but by *who* they represent. And it makes me wonder: *What name am I wearing and reflecting to the world? What will I be known for?*

In Exodus 28, the priestly garments are detailed for us. Worn by the High Priest whenever he entered the sanctuary, these garments carried dual symbolism. Adorned with two onyx stones that were each engraved with six names of the sons of Israel (vv.9-10), and a "breastplate of judgment" set with twelve stones (vv.17-21), they first represented the twelve tribes of Israel. As the High Priest stepped behind the veil to offer atoning sacrifices for the sin of the nation, he did so as their representative, wearing their very names in the presence of God. But he also represented God.

When the High Priest addressed the nations, he wore a plain white turban with a gold plate engraved with the words "Holy to the Lord" fastened to his forehead (v.38). This was his seal, a trademark of sorts indicating he was dedicated to the Lord alone and pledged to serve no other.

While such elaborate garments may seem odd today, God used this distinctive clothing to set His spiritual leaders apart from the other Israelites. As a nation, they lived with a continual reminder of the importance of the priestly work. It was also a foreshadowing of Jesus, the "great high priest" (Hebrews 4:14), the One who would carry out God's plan of atonement in true holiness and perfection.

Under the old covenant in the Old Testament, the priests were derived from the tribe of Levi—they could only be descendants of Aaron. People were not able to choose if they became priests, God chose for them. In the New Testament under the new covenant, Jesus was the High Priest called by God (Hebrew 4:14) who through His sacrifice, called us all to be a royal priesthood and holy nation (1 Peter 2:9). Chosen by God, through the sacrifice of Jesus we, too, have now received priestly status.

One of the most significant roles of the priest was to first minister to God. We are called to do the same: to build a lifestyle of worship and relationship with the One that appointed us, submitting to the transforming power of Holy Spirit who changes us from the inside out. Renewed in the image of Christ, we are called to represent God to the people we meet daily.

In the presence of God, the priest represented a nation that sinned and had fallen short of God's glory. However, before the people, the priest represented the immeasurable grace and love of God. As twenty-first century priests, we, too, need to understand that "all have sinned and fall short of the glory of God" (Romans 3:23), yet through Jesus' blood, God is now present within us. The blood of the Lamb protects us from death; the veil is torn, and we no longer need to enter the presence of God in fear of our lives.

We will never fully grasp the depth of the love, grace, and mercy of God. Yet as imperfect people, redeemed by the blood of Jesus, we can wear the name of the Lord with pride and honour, seeking to represent His love daily to those that have not yet experienced His goodness. What a responsibility and privilege it is to wear our 'priestly garments' as a reflection of this Living Hope!

What will you be known for? How are you 'wearing' God's name? Are there garments of the world you need to take off so that you can put on His character and love?

DAY TWENTY-NINE

Simple Intimacy

NICOLE O'MEARA

Exodus 29

I watched as four of my classmates, dressed in suits and ties, placed a wreath at the foot of the Tomb of the Unknown Soldier. A soldier in dress uniform then marched the wreath to the tomb and saluted. Despite the crowd, I heard the whisper of his feet and a few songbirds in the fields of white crosses around us. Within minutes, the ceremony was over and the crowd dispersed in quiet reverence.

Pageantry in reverent ceremonies is important. When a bride enters a chapel, the organ plays and guests stand. In a royal parade, the King waves and servants bow. And in Exodus 29, we witness God's design for the pageantry of the consecration of the priests: white garments, blood sprinkled, and the pleasant aroma of burning meat filling the air. In each situation, the ceremony, with all its rituals, does not change the people. The bride is still a woman in love. The King is still a man in charge. The priests are still sinners in need of atonement. But the ceremony gives those of us in the crowd a clear sense of the gravity of the moment. God desired that this moment should be remembered and honoured for what He was doing: creating a way to dwell with His people.

The rich theology behind the consecration of the priests has much to teach us about the seriousness of being made holy before our holy God. Note that the first sacrifice Moses made was the sin offering. Before the priests could begin their work; before they could meet God at the entrance to the Tabernacle, their sin needed to be atoned. They needed to be made holy, purified of their sin. The same is true for us. Our sin must be cleansed before we can meet with God.

Sacrifices are an interesting means for us to connect with God. They are messy, time consuming, and need daily repetition. It is not the obvious method for cleansing. Yet, it is the method God designed for the priests as a foreshadow of the ultimate sacrifice Christ made for us. Only after our sin has been forgiven can we meet with God guilt-free. Thankfully Christ made a way! His death on the cross atoned for our sin; He was our ultimate and complete sin offering.

But He didn't just make a way for us to meet with God, He also made a way for us to be *used* by God in the world, just like the priests of Israel. 1 Peter 2:5 says, "You yourselves like living stones are being built up as a spiritual house, to be a holy priesthood, to offer spiritual sacrifices acceptable to God through Jesus Christ" (ESV). Thankfully, we are not sprinkled with anointing oil mixed with ram's blood. (*Would Oxi-Clean get 'those' stains out?*) Instead, we have been made priests through the blood of Christ. As we read in Revelation 1:5-6, ". . .and from Jesus Christ the faithful witness, the firstborn of the dead, and the ruler of kings on earth. To him who loves us and has freed us from our sins by his blood and made us a kingdom, priests to his God and Father" (ESV).

The word 'priest' and the role of a priest may be unfamiliar in our modern lives, so it can be difficult to consider ourselves as priests. Thankfully, in our priesthood, we can take comfort knowing we do not have to make daily animal sacrifices in order to meet with God. We can perform our own private ceremonies such as preparing a hot cup of coffee, bringing our Bible, journal, and favourite pen to a comfortable chair, or watching the sunrise as we recite a psalm. Simple. Intimate. Holy. Christ has torn down the barrier. Let us all be glad.

What 'private ceremonies' help you to connect with God? How could you be more intentional about weaving these into your daily rhythms?

DAY THIRTY

Ginosko

EMILY TYLER

Exodus 30

During the Covid-19 epidemic there were rules in place with respect to how we were to interact with others. There was a strong emphasis on washing hands, staying clean, and keeping our distance—all mandated with a view to keeping people safe. Here in chapter 30, we see certain similarities: The priests are given specific rules to enable them to be in the presence of a holy God "so that they will not die" (v.20).

One of the hardest things for many during the strict lockdowns was the enforced isolation from one another. God evidently feels the same way about us as this chapter is bookended with His desire to meet with His people (vv.6 and 36). The Hebrew verb *yaad* means 'to meet at an appointment' and the Septuagint equivalent *ginosko* means 'to know by experience'.

When we meet with God, we come to experience and know Him.

The Altar of Incense was the closest item of furniture in the Tabernacle to the Holy of Holies, where God resided, and its sole purpose was the burning of incense. Throughout Scripture, incense symbolises prayer. David asked that his "prayer be set before [God] like incense" (Psalm 141:2a), and John records "golden bowls full of incense" as being "the prayers of God's people" in Revelation 5:8.

But not just *anyone* could go and offer up their prayers here. Before approaching the golden altar, as it is otherwise known, the High Priest would first need to deal with the bronze altar where the sacrifice for sins would be made. Then he would encounter the bronze basin to cleanse himself (v.19) before offering incense twice daily (vv.7-8). This was the moment to pray for the community and speak with God (Luke 1:10).

This pattern of sacrifice, cleansing, and prayer is still relevant to us today as we seek to have meaningful intimacy with God. Unlike the priests, we can approach Him with confidence because Jesus made the once-for-all sacrifice and shed His blood to bring us complete atonement. That part is complete. Yet, there is still a need for cleansing before we approach God. Only those with "clean hands and a pure heart" (Psalm 24:4a) will offer prayers with a pleasing aroma. Intercession was a function reserved only for the priests, yet now, as priests ourselves (1 Peter 2:9), when we repeatedly confess our sin we are promised cleansing "from all unrighteousness" (1 John 1:9).

After sacrifice and cleansing, the burning of incense could take place. The perpetual offering of incense would have filled the whole Tabernacle with its sweet aroma. God's house was to be a "house of prayer" (Isaiah 56:7), a place filled with worship and supplication. And now, as carriers of His Holy Spirit, we living temples are equally called to fill our lives with a continuous offering of prayer (1 Corinthians 6:19; 1 Thessalonians 5:17; Luke 18:1). It is prayer that leads us into continual and perfect intimacy with the Father and allows us to know and experience Him fully as we are fully known.

As we understand the great privilege of having this relational intimacy with our holy God, let's approach Him with confidence *and* respect. The oil and incense in the Tabernacle was holy and set apart (vv.31-38) to be used solely by the priests for the purpose of burning incense before the Lord. Our prayers are to be equally sacrosanct in bringing God glory. Jesus Himself warned against using prayer for anything other than intimacy with the Father (Matthew 6 and 23).

Above all, God desperately desires continual communion with His people, and He's done everything necessary through His Son to make it possible. As our perfect High Priest (Hebrews 4:14), Jesus models what it is to constantly intercede on our behalf before the Father (Hebrews 7:25; 9:24). As we look to Him, may we, too, *ginosko* with God—experiencing the fullness and beauty of deep and permanent relational intimacy with Him.

What does it look like for you to become a 'house of prayer'? Is there anyone or thing that you sense God is asking you to commit to regularly praying for? Make a plan and be obedient to this prompting.

Holy Rest

ELLIE DI JULIO

Exodus 31

After six chapters of exhaustive detail on the construction of the Tabernacle and its many parts, we find ourselves breathing a sigh of relief. Finally, we can get on with the story. And while it's tempting to breeze through these verses to the juicy part about the golden calf, in doing so we would risk missing a key design pattern for life.

While this chapter appears to be two distinct halves, it's no coincidence that God repeats the commandment to observe the Sabbath—to cease all work and be with Him for a day—right on the heels of a complex set of moral and architectural instructions. As the master craftsman who created humans in the first place, He knows exactly how easy it is for us to succumb to work, to fall under the spell of a vision to the exclusion of all else. *How much easier would it have been for the artisans tasked with constructing God's own home on earth?* By restating and elaborating on the purpose of the Sabbath— and the consequences for breaking it—God reminds His people that without holy rest they will surely perish (vv.14-17).

This reminder transports us all the way back to Genesis 2 when God rests from the work of Creation, setting apart the seventh day and deeming it holy (vv.2-3). It's actually the first thing humans observe their Father doing: resting. Laying aside the work of His hands, the Lord chooses to be present with His children and enjoy the good world He has made. It's not that He didn't have a zillion things to do—Creation had just started, after all—but He made a purposeful choice to model holy rest to us as part of His personal pattern of existence.

Israel took this to heart. They not only constructed their week around the Sabbath but their years, decades, and lifetimes, observing patterns of seventh-day rest in larger concentric circles of festivals, forgiveness, and fallowness (Leviticus 25:1-55). It's a testament to how seriously God takes this command that not keeping it is a primary reason for the Babylonian Exile (2 Chronicles 36:21). One way or another, Sabbath rest must come because it is God's own rhythm woven into our nature as His children.

In response, priests and scribes begin to outline precisely how to keep the Sabbath. By the time Jesus arrives on the scene, there are thirty-nine categories and hundreds of rules delineating what one cannot do as 'work' on the day of rest. The Sabbath, a blessing originally given to create space for God's children to intimately dwell with Him, had become a punishing legalistic system.

One that Jesus redeems.

To us, the Lord of the Sabbath proclaims: "Are you tired? Worn out? Burned out on religion? Come to me. Get away with me and you'll recover your life. I'll show you how to take a real rest. Walk with me and work with me—watch how I do it. Learn the unforced rhythms of grace. I won't lay anything heavy or ill-fitting on you. Keep company with me and you'll learn to live freely and lightly" (Matthew 11:28-30 MSG).

In our hectic modern lives filled with meetings, sports, ministry, and laundry, we can barely carve out time to attend church, much less stop working and simply be with God. We grind ourselves into exhausted dust, micromanaging our world until we find we're all alone, isolated from our community and our God—a dangerous place to be when there's a lion on the loose (1 Peter 5:8).

Sabbath rest is both a warning and a command. It is also a gift—an invitation written by the hand of the Father, sealed by the Son, and empowered by the Spirit. Because of Christ, no longer is it a weekly or yearly retreat from the busyness of life but a daily rhythm of grace; a way of living that moves at the pace of *shalom*, dwelling ever in the presence of the Lord, and trusting that He will take care of what cannot be done by the work of our hands.

Come to Him, you who are weary and burdened, and He will give you rest.

Where do you need to practice rest so that you might draw closer to Jesus? What obstacles might you need to be aware of and what steps can you take to ensure that they don't prevent you from receiving God's gift of rest?

DAY THIRTY-TWO
Righteous
JENNA MARIE MASTERS

Exodus 32

Sometimes I imagine picking up the broken pieces of my life and clumsily offering them to God. I hope that He will piece them back together, making something beautiful. Well, *almost* beautiful—if it wasn't for all those cracks showing through this glued-together version of me, I would be stunning. Although I imagine God has put me back together into some kind of functioning vessel, I can still see all the jagged pottery bits trying to cling together gracefully. I suspect that one little wisp of wind will send me crashing to the ground, and I will shatter all over again.

But if we belong to King Jesus, this viewpoint isn't biblical. Second Corinthians 5:17 teaches us, "Therefore, if anyone is in Christ, he is a new creation. The old has passed away; behold, the new has come" (ESV).

The *new* has come. It does not say, "If anyone is in Christ, He will put them back together."

If this is how we view ourselves, we'll have trouble. When God leads us through a desert, we may fall back into our old ways of life like the Israelites, their faith slipping out through cracks they think God has forgotten to repair.

Their actions in this chapter stem from a spirit that has been crushed by slavery, even though their bodies are now free. They grow impatient waiting for God's plan to unfold, complaining that Moses is taking too long to come down from the mountain (v.1). Old practices promised false security, so they fashion a god with tools, as they'd done for years (v.4), and lament the food they ate as slaves.

Still seeing themselves as slaves, they would rather mix the life they knew in captivity with the new life God was offering them. But if you combine the old with the new, it isn't purely new. We are encouraged to "forget the former things; do not dwell on the past!" God is doing a new thing, and He longs for us to perceive it! (Isaiah 43:18-19).

God wanted this so badly for the Israelites, and they missed it. Even after Moses so selflessly pleads to God, "Please forgive their sin—but if not, then blot me out of the book you have written" (Exodus 32:32), they suffer great consequences.

All but two of these Israelites end up missing out on the Promised Land because most refused to trust in the new life God was offering. They allowed past decisions and experiences to define them, content to imagine their lives as a repaired vase on the shelf—as I once did.

But we are not simply the products of a clumsy repair job, although Satan is quick to assure us that being repaired is enough—even more than we deserve. It is true: A repaired life *is* more than what we deserve. But Romans 6:4 tells us, "We were therefore buried with him through baptism into death in order that, just as Christ was raised from the dead through the glory of the Father, we too may live a new life."

Who are we to be so bold, to dash and diminish the work of the cross, and even more so, to belittle the power of the resurrection?

We will never understand the self-sacrificing, all-consuming love of our Saviour. But let us try to understand the foolishness in viewing ourselves as *repaired* instead of *righteous*, or longing to be enslaved when we have been made free. For "it is for freedom that Christ has set us free" (Galatians 5:1a).

In what ways are you clinging to an old version of yourself? Invite Holy Spirit to empower you to truly believe that you are who Jesus says you are as you declare, "I am in Christ and I am a new creation. The old has passed and the new has come."

DAY THIRTY-THREE

Seek His Heart

MAZHAR KEFALI

Exodus 33

This chapter paints a revealing portrait of the differences between Moses—a man who desired an intimate relationship with God and wanted to grow in his insight of the Lord and His ways—and the Israelites, who preferred to remain at a distance, seeking God only for the benefits He could offer them.

In the opening verses, we see Yahweh reaffirming His promise to Moses and Israel concerning their destiny. Only, this time, the rules of engagement have changed. He will still be present with them on their journey but instead of His direct presence, He will send an angel before them (vv.1-3). A clear reason for this is given: The people of Israel had rebelled against Him, and due to their lack of patience concerning the pace and process of Yahweh's timing and ways, they ended up manufacturing idols to worship, causing them to sin and creating separation between them and God.

When God does not work in the ways we think He ought to, we risk focusing our faith and attention on material indicators instead of trusting in His promise and character. His ways are different to ours, and given that He inhabits eternity, He is the only one who knows the end from the beginning (Isaiah 46:8; 55:6-9; 57:15).

Moses, however, exhibited a whole different heart and disposition from the "stiffnecked people" he was called to lead. Because of his longing for a deep and personal relationship with Yahweh, the Lord spoke to Moses "face to face" (v.11), like speaking with a friend. Moses had become a humbled man during his forty years as a shepherd, learning that the nature and ways of Yahweh were far beyond anything he could ever comprehend in his humanity. As one who feared the Lord, He took the "teach me. . . show me" posture of heart that God responds to (see Psalm 25), because he desired to know Him and receive His favour (v.13).

Yet, while Moses had confidence in the promise and character of Yahweh, he could not bear the thought that the presence of God would not go with them (vv.12-16). He knew that God's very presence was a sign that Yahweh was with them and would 'distinguish' and 'mark them out' as His people (vv.15-16).

In the Old Testament, the presence of God was external, manifest in objective ways. As New Testament believers, the overwhelming reality is that the presence of God is within us through the indwelling Holy Spirit.

In verse 17, Yahweh affirms that He *will* reveal His presence to Moses. Given this positive response, Moses takes his request a step further and asks Him for a full revelation of His glory (v.18). The Hebrew word that describes God's glory here conveys the full expression of His 'honour, splendour, dignity, and reputation'.

The reply Moses receives reveals the absolute purity and holiness of God, and the gulf between Him and us in our sinful humanity. He is eternal and immortal, and we are creatures of time and mortality. This is made clear when Moses is told that "no one" can see the fullness of the glory of God, face to face, and live. His absolute holiness is all consuming (Hebrews 12:28-29). He is invisible to the human eye and dwells in unapproachable light (1 Timothy 1:17; 1 John 4:12). The Scriptures are clear that the only one who has ever seen the Father is the Son (John 1:18; 6:46).

The closest Moses would get to experiencing the glory of God was "seeing [God's] back" (v.23). This expression in Hebrew conveys the sense of 'the after effects of His radiant glory, which has just passed by'. Through offering Moses this glimpse of His glory—an expression of His goodness portrayed through His mercy and compassion—we see that God reveals Himself to those who have the heart and patience to pursue Him.

Where have you become focused on and distracted by material outcomes? Take a moment to repent and centre your heart on the Lord. As you seek Him, what truth is He speaking that you need to hold on to today?

Surprised by Mercy

NICOLE O'MEARA

Exodus 34

I remember when I met my first Honours English teacher in high school. My first impression of Mrs. Horner was a strict, no-nonsense, grey-haired woman. After our first class, I was sure she was going to be boring, maybe even scary. But as we travelled through the school year together, I learned she was also kind and unusually patient—a characteristic developed from decades of teaching freshmen.

For my first book report, I chose a novel more suited for adventurous boys than a nerdy-girl like me. I struggled to read it. When it came time to turn in a report, I knew I wasn't ready. I deserved whatever consequences stern Mrs. Horner handed down.

And she did. The bold red comments on my pitiful report made me want to crawl under my desk and disappear. But it got worse. "Nicole, would you please stay after the bell? I want to speak with you." I dreaded the end of class. *How much more needed to be said?* I didn't follow the book report instructions. I was ashamed. I didn't belong in the class.

Her gentle tone increased my guilt. "Why did you choose that book?"

"It was the only one we owned from your list."

"I think you might like a different kind of book," she said. "May I make a suggestion?"

Curiosity temporarily soothed my shame. I watched as she walked to her bookshelf, took out a small blue book, and handed it to me. "Try this."

And with that, I was dismissed. She said nothing about my failed book report or about not belonging in an honours level class. She gave out no extra punishments—just a book that, as it turned out, I loved. I still have it. In a moment when I deserved punishment, I received mercy instead, and it changed my trajectory forever.

That's the thing about mercy. It comes when we least expect it, and it changes us. The Israelites have blown it with the golden calf. They know it the moment Moses comes down the mountain. God's judgement on them is no surprise. But His mercy is.

When Israel could reasonably expect their just God to hand down justice, what does God choose to tell Moses about Himself in that moment? He proclaims Himself Jehovah, God Almighty. And then, from His own goodness, He describes His mercy, something the Israelites desperately need after their ghastly unfaithfulness. And it's something we need, too, for we are not unlike the Israelites, seeking our own idols when God seems distant.

God describes His mercy in several ways: "Compassionate and gracious. . . slow to anger, abounding in love and faithfulness, maintaining love to thousands, and forgiving wickedness, rebellion and sin. Yet he does not leave the guilty unpunished; he punishes the children and their children for the sin of the parents to the third and fourth generation" (vv.6-7). This mercy was given to Israel, and is given to us today, through no effort on our part, simply out of God's good pleasure.

God wants His children to understand He is not a one-sided deity, simply waiting for the moment He can throw down His judgement like lightning bolts. No, He has many characteristics including love. God *loves* His children. His judgement comes out of His love and for our good, redirecting us away from the dangers of sin like a well-earned failing grade redirected this student. Here, God wanted the Israelites to notice that even His judgement is a demonstration of His mercy.

In Exodus 34:6, when God proclaims His name, He does it 'in transitu'—while passing by. Similarly today, He gives us increasing knowledge of Himself and His character through the words He gives us in Scripture while we journey through life together. Our jealous God wants our full devotion but it is sweeter when we give our devotion with *full* knowledge of the One in whom we love. Let's be thankful that though God is so much more than we can ever fully grasp, He will continue to reveal more of Himself to us along the way.

Humbly present yourself before the Lord today. Thank Him for His mercy and the many ways He has revealed Himself to You already, then ask Him to lead you into a deeper understanding of who He is. What is He showing you?

DAY THIRTY-FIVE

There is Always Treasure

ASHLEY KELLY

Exodus 35

Growing up as a pastor's kid, the stories in the Old Testament about the amazing works of God—Noah and the ark, Joseph and the coat of many colors, the splitting of the Red Sea, David and Goliath— were as familiar to me as any common bedtime story. I knew the details, I knew the outcomes, and I knew who always showed Himself mighty. I'm grateful for this strong foundation formed at such a young age, but, truthfully, it presented a few obstacles later down the road when I began digging deeper into Scripture. I tended to read through familiar portions of the Old Testament as though I knew all there was to know. My critical thinking skills took a back seat to what I already *knew* to be true.

As I have grown—both in age and spiritual maturity—I have learned the necessity and beauty of slowly reading these familiar passages of the Bible. The stories I grew up hearing are full of wisdom and revelations of our wonderful God, and offer so much more than I could ever have imagined as a child. Slow, thoughtful reading—like we are doing through this study—reveals countless treasures.

One key strategy to encourage slow, thoughtful reading that I often employ is asking questions—questions that most likely would not arise if it wasn't for that slower pace. For example, in today's reading, I found myself wondering *how* the Israelites obtain all the gold, silver, fine linens, purple yarns, brooches, and earrings that they willingly offer for the building of the Tabernacle (vv.5-9). *Where did these treasures come from?* These are former slaves, nomadically roaming the desert without a place to call their own. Surely former slaves wouldn't have ample gold, silver, and jewels just lying around.

It appears they willingly gave their treasures as their hearts stirred and moved them. This is repeated no less than six times! And this should be celebrated and praised. God is the One stirring them.

They are participating in God's beautiful plan to construct a way for Him to be near His people! But I want to know where their treasure came from—*don't you?*

The only logical origin of these cherished and costly items is found earlier in Exodus 12. The final plague so devastated the Egyptians that they practically begged the Israelites to leave. In their grief and desperation, the Egyptians agreed to give the Israelites all they asked as long as they departed in haste. *What did they request?* They "asked the Egyptians for silver and gold jewellery and for clothing. . . Thus they plundered the Egyptians" (vv.35-36 ESV).

It seems as though the very items that are to be used to fashion and form the dwelling place of the Lord come from a place of great heartache for the Israelites where they experienced slavery and bondage. Their troubled past paved a way for their future blessing. Not a blessing consisting of material things or further treasures but the very presence of the Lord. Even during times of difficulty, hardship, and oppression (whether physically, mentally, or spiritually), God was working to provide for His people's future needs.

There is treasure to be plundered in every situation—good or bad. There is wisdom to be learned, growth to be had, and resources to be imparted. Our God is limitless, and far be it from us to be the ones to try and limit Him. God provided a way for His plan to come to fruition even when the Israelites couldn't see that far ahead, and He still does the same for us today.

When it comes to studying Scripture, slowing down our pace and reading thoughtfully can lead us to uncover nuggets of truth about our God that we may otherwise have missed. This passage itself is powerful, but digging deeper adds a new depth to our understanding of the goodness of God and His ultimate plan. Having familiarity with the stories of the Bible is all well and good until it hinders our ability to learn all we can about the One who authored these stories in the first place. So let's delight in slowly digging deeper into God's Word—and uncovering new treasures along the way!

How have you seen God bring treasure from a place of heartache and pain? Where do you need to believe afresh that blessings lie ahead for you?

_____

_____

_____

_____

_____

_____

_____

_____

_____

_____

_____

_____

_____

_____

_____

_____

_____

_____

_____

_____

_____

_____

DAY THIRTY-SIX
Gifted
VICKI BENTLEY

Exodus 36

"I have a problem Mummy," my seven-year-old declared one morning. "I've finished designing my game, but I don't know what to do next!"

My daughter is a born inventor. Her brain swirls with grand plans and ideas for video games, board games, books, and toys. Her ability to make these fabulous blueprints a reality, however, tends to be limited by her skill-level; her vision is often frustrated by her incapacity to follow through with her designs in any practical way.

Here in Exodus chapter thirty-six, we see no such conundrum. God has carefully communicated His vision for the Tabernacle to Moses and the Israelites, and now it's 'go-time'. And to avoid any confusion or hesitation over who should begin this divine work and how, God makes it crystal clear that He has already made the preparations necessary to put His plan into action.

Moses tells the people: "The Lord has gifted Bezalel, Oholiab, and the other skilled craftsmen with wisdom and ability to perform any task involved in building the sanctuary. Let them construct and furnish the Tabernacle, just as the Lord has commanded" (v.1 NLT). They, along with "all the others who were especially gifted by the Lord. . . were eager to get to work" (v.2 NLT).

What an honour it must have been for these men to be called by name and given this holy assignment. They were chosen because of their excellence as craftsmen and as designers (Exodus 35:35), but Scripture is clear that these skills were not self-made, but gifted by the Lord to accomplish *His* purposes. And as His people, we are granted the same honour today.

1 Peter 4:10 tells us that, "God has given each of you a gift. . . Use them well to serve one another" (1 Peter 4:10). Perhaps the gift God

has blessed you with doesn't seem all that important, impressive, or spiritual, but be encouraged that *every* good gift is from God (James 1:17), and He has assigned them with great intentionality and purpose in order to do "good works, which He prepared in advance for us to do" (Ephesians 2:10). Even if the task seems beyond our own ability, we can trust that if God gives us a vision, He will also equip us with the necessary skills or labour required to finish the job.

It's important to highlight, however, that while this construction was getting underway, the rest of the Israelites were not resting on their laurels, simply content to observe their peers doing the work. No, they were busy gathering the materials God had requested as an offering. In fact, such was their willingness to provide what was needed for the completion of the Tabernacle, Moses actually had to tell them, "We have enough!" for their "contributions were more than enough to complete the whole project" (vv.6-7 NLT).

Imagine if next time your church asked for a donation or offering, the response from the congregation far outweighed what was needed. *How might our churches and communities be transformed if we each gave generously and willingly with that very same spirit of eager abundance?*

The opening verses of this chapter should encourage us all that we each play a key role in the work God has called us to. Whether we are directed to perform a specific spiritual, professional or practical role, or are simply asked to offer what little we have for the work of the Kingdom, Scripture tells us to "work willingly at whatever [we] do, as though [we] were working for the Lord rather than for people" (Colossians 3:23).

God loves a cheerful giver (2 Corinthians 9:7), and He has gifted us abundantly. So let's follow the Israelites' example and be people who fully offer ourselves and all our God-given talents, time, and tithes with eagerness so that "everything [we] do will bring glory to God through Jesus Christ" (1 Peter 4:11 NLT). He is the Architect, after all, and what an honour it is to be trusted with a role in His Kingdom construction.

What gifts has God given you? Spend some time sitting with Holy Spirit, how is He inviting you to develop them and use them to serve the Lord and His people?

_____

_____

_____

_____

_____

_____

_____

_____

_____

_____

_____

_____

_____

_____

_____

_____

_____

_____

_____

_____

_____

_____

_____

A Chest Full of Hope

TABITHA MEGLICH

Exodus 37

It was little more than a simple wooden trunk, but that hope chest held the place of honour at the foot of my bed through the better part of my teens. Many an hour was spent tenderly rearranging its contents and revelling in the sense of accomplishment each time another treasure was tucked away.

Nestled among my current furnishings is a slightly more refined version—a flea-market find crafted from cherry wood and lined with aromatic cedar. Inside the cover, inscribed along the lower edge, are the endearing words, "Received for my birthday from my sweetheart John. June 20, 1929." Nearly one hundred years old, this antique speaks to the heart of this cherished tradition.

A hope chest is exactly what the name implies: the curation of special items by a young woman in the hope and anticipation of intimate, covenant love. And as I read about the Tabernacle furnishings in Exodus, I am struck by the fact that God gave His people something special to be their own divine hope chest of sorts. Designed to curate the most sacred articles, the Ark, which comes from the Hebrew word *aron* meaning 'box' or 'chest', was referred to in Scripture by three names—the *Ark of the Covenant* (Joshua 3:6), the *Ark of the Testimony* (Exodus 25:22), and the *Ark of God* (2 Samuel 6:2). Symbolic of God's heavenly throne, this was where the Spirit and glory of Jehovah rested among His people (Exodus 25:10-22).

The Ark housed three historic artefacts, specifically chosen by the Lord, that bore testimony to His faithfulness to His covenant with Israel (Exodus 25:21):

Stone tablets bearing the Ten Commandments: A testimony to God's holiness and a reminder that man will inevitably break the Covenant Law and is in need of a Saviour (Romans 3:20).

A jar of manna: A testimony to God's sustaining provision in the wilderness, supernaturally preserved (Exodus 16:32).

Aaron's staff: This lifeless staff budded, blossomed and produced almonds as confirmation that Aaron's line was the chosen priesthood (Numbers 17:1-11).

I have to imagine that Israel's relationship with this chest was complicated. The Ark of the Covenant was both a wonder to behold and a fearsome thing. Its very presence was assurance to Israel that the Lord was still with them, despite their endlessly wayward heart. Yet, it was a paragon of Yahweh's glory that demanded reverence, consecration, and absolute adherence to strict protocols that, if violated, meant being struck down. The cherubim standing guard over the mercy seat and the Ark's location within the Holy of Holies, shrouded behind a veil and far beyond their reach, was a poignant reminder of their unworthiness and magnified the sin that separated them from the presence of a holy God. Yet, the Ark was more than that. So. Much. More

This sacred chest held the treasure of a promise—anticipation of the fulfilment of a longing; the longing in every human soul for intimacy and covenant love. The items within foreshadowed a future when the promised seed of Eve would come and all would be made right. A future when the throne of God would be approachable and the intimacy intended with humanity would be restored. Ultimately, the Ark was a sacred chest burgeoning with hope—hope that one day the *Covenant Keeper* would fulfil the Law on our behalf. The true manna, the incorruptible *Bread of Life* (John 6:23-25), would come to satisfy the hunger of the human soul. The *Life-Giver* would be the first to be reborn from death unto life (Revelation 1:5).

Is it any wonder that King David danced joyfully in the streets as the Ark of the Covenant was victoriously paraded through the gates of Jerusalem?

As followers of Jesus, we are living testimonies of the fulfilment of that hope through the New Covenant sealed by His blood (Hebrews 9:2-5). Though flawed and broken—vessels of clay unworthy by our very nature to be in the presence of a holy God—every believer, cleansed by the blood of the Lamb, is the dwelling place of His Spirit. By His grace, you and I are the bearers of this eternal, blessed hope.

Build your own 'Chest of Hope'. What testimonies of God's past faithfulness do you need to place in it? What promises from God do you need to believe will yet bud and bloom? Invite Holy Spirit to stir fresh expectancy within you.

DAY THIRTY-EIGHT

Mirror, Mirror
EMILY TYLER

Exodus 38

My mother tells me that if she lost sight of me in a department store when I was little, all she had to do to find me was to locate the nearest mirror. There I would be, standing in front of it—gazing at myself, pulling poses, and generally absorbed in my own image.

There's a small detail in today's chapter about the bronze basin that we read about earlier (Exodus 30). It was made "from the mirrors of the women who served at the entrance to the tent of meeting" (Exodus 38:8).

Mirrors in the days of the Tabernacle were not as we know them now. These mirrors would have been made from any material that could be polished to create a reflection—in this case, bronze. These particular ones are likely to have come from Egypt which was well-known for its creation of cosmetic artefacts, in particular, beautiful and valuable mirrors. Hammered metal, almost always in an elliptical shape, would have been highly polished before being inserted into a handle made of wood, ivory, stone, or metal. These handles were invariably carved with different representations of Egyptian gods and other idols.

If the women serving at the temple were anything like me (I can still be known to check my reflection when out walking past a shop window), they would have been looking at themselves in these mirrors with reasonable frequency.

The problem is, we reflect what we look at.

Perhaps this small, seemingly inconsequential verse actually leads us to surrender and sacrifice that which distracts us from looking at and worshipping God. We are all naturally bent towards self-worship and need to learn how to stop looking at idols and worthless 'treasure' that cannot make us beautiful. These women would flock

121

to the tent of meeting and assemble for worship much like military troops would gather for their duties. These women were prepared to devote themselves to Tabernacle service; they were prepared to hold nothing back.

To do so, the women surrendered what they were holding onto, the things they were looking to for self-worth, significance, and security. These mirrors would have been their prized possessions and they willingly chose to lay down what they held most dear—laying down the distraction of self and surrendering it in worship for the benefit of not only themselves but the whole community.

We all want to be beautiful. But the problem comes when we start looking at ourselves to discover that beauty. From the beginning of time, we were made in the image and likeness of God (Genesis 1:26). We have been intrinsically, fearfully, and wonderfully made (Psalm 139). If we reflect what we look at, then we need to get better at looking to the truth of God's Word for our value and worth.

We need to reflect Jesus.

Moses' face would physically glow and radiate after spending time in God's presence (Exodus 34:29-35) to the point that he needed a veil to shield those around him even though that glory was destined to fade away. But we are not like Moses for we have Holy Spirit giving us life and "far greater glory" that will remain forever (2 Corinthians 3:7-18).

We have unfettered access to the One who will make us truly and deeply beautiful, free from the world's definition and self-carved idols. "For the Lord is the Spirit, and wherever the Spirit of the Lord is, there is freedom. . . And the Lord—who is the Spirit—makes us more and more like him as we are changed into his glorious image" (2 Corinthians 3:17 and 18b NLT).

May we lay down the idols we hold so tightly as an act of surrendered worship. Let us be free from looking at that which provides a dim, distorted image, and instead look to the One who promises "perfect clarity" (1 Corinthians 13:12), a glorious and free future!

Spend some time beholding Jesus. (You may wish to use a passage like Isaiah 53 or Philippians 2:6-11) What do you notice about Him? Invite Holy Spirit to empower you to reflect this attribute of Jesus today.

DAY THIRTY-NINE
Holy to the Lord
SHELLEY JOHNSTON

Exodus 39

Inspection Day has arrived! All the instructions have been given; all the work has been completed. Now the leader of this new nation walks through the last stack of items for examination. With his clipboard-like tablet, Moses checks the boxes of the final inventory list—the priestly garments.

Ephod: check.
Breastpiece: check.
Robe of linen with a hem of pomegranates and bells: check.
Tunic, turban, headband, undergarments, and sash: check, check, check, check, check.
Gold plate (dramatic pause).

It's here that my mind visualises Moses lifting the engraved plate to read its inscription, "HOLY TO THE LORD" (v.30). I imagine a lump rising in his throat as he wraps his fingers around the shiny medallion and mumbles a prayer, "Lord, let it be so."

Because Moses knows 'holy'.

He is also familiar with the wickedness that lurks within humanity (Exodus 32:1). So, in my mind's eye, he prays that with these hallowed clothes, the priests will embody holiness as they serve in humble reverence of Yahweh. He prays the people under his care will embrace the sacredness of the place they're about to construct because it is the man-made tent God Almighty has chosen to enter into in order to dwell amongst His people again.

Whether or not the people have fully grasped the sacred and holy nature of the task set before them, we are told they have obeyed every command of God. And Moses blesses them for it (v.43).

My own lack of understanding of what holy means struck me

124

most violently the day I visited the Church of the Holy Sepulcher in Jerusalem. I watched with fascination and curiosity as people kneeled next to a slab of marble, rocking back and forth in fevered worship because *this* was the place Jesus' dead body once lay.

After making my way through the church, I stopped again to watch the continuing drama unfold at the burial slab when a woman caught my eye. Sobbing, she lay as prostrate as possible across her corner of the slab uninhibited in her display of love. And, it struck me.

She knows holy. And I do not.

This moment gifted me with a vision of genuine reverence. The woman's display of adoration for Jesus paints a picture of how I imagine Moses is feeling on this special day because they both perceive the depths of divine holiness.

We can know holy, too.

Each time we remember that Jesus, the Lamb of God, has poured out His blood to sanctify us, we can worship Him in awe and gratitude. When our spirits are moved by a work of His Spirit, we can allow the sanctity of the moment to expand our souls. We can also receive His love, giving it space to awaken within us the truth that we are His. And, we can be assured of our own holiness because He is holy (1 Peter 1:15-16).

Just as God's presence would fill the Tabernacle, Christ's Spirit dwells within us. We are God's temple; we embody His holiness. Like Moses, we can understand holy because we have a relationship with the Holy One. Our entry into God's presence is through Christ. We're given access by our faith—not a checklist of laws. Like Aaron and his brothers, we enter God's presence as His royal priests (1 Peter 2:9), but instead of linen garments, we are adorned in robes of righteousness (Isaiah 61:10).

So, imagine yourself, God's beloved and chosen one, putting on your new garments of compassion, kindness, humility, gentleness, and patience (Colossians 3:12). Then, as you reach up to touch the gold plate dangling from your turban, remember *you* are "HOLY TO THE LORD."

Pause and visualise yourself clothed in these priestly garments. As you put them on, invite Holy Spirit to stir within you a fresh revelation of the holiness of God, embracing the awe and wonder of all Jesus has done to make us holy to the Lord.

_____

_____

_____

_____

_____

_____

_____

_____

_____

_____

_____

_____

_____

_____

_____

_____

_____

_____

_____

_____

A Faithful Guide

AMBER PALMER

Exodus 40

It's been one year since the Iraelites left their lives of slavery and headed into the wilderness to follow God. Life outside of Egypt did not generally meet the Israelites' expectations, and what they anticipated would be an easier life ended up being more of a challenge. Blessings quickly turned to burdens, relief turned to discomfort, and fear of the unknown stole the joy of expectancy from their hearts. Their journey had fallen foul of their human nature thus far and they grumbled and complained their way through the desert, making sinful choices against God and His plans for them.

Even though the Israelites' choices were not always on par with what God intended for them, they did at least manage to demonstrate perfect obedience in the building of the Tabernacle, and Exodus 40 is when all their hard work and heart work come together. It's the moment we've all been waiting for—when each piece that was independently crafted becomes dependent on one another to create a holy space for God to enter.

Each piece of precious metal, wood, and fabric beheld their own beauty and purpose, but God needed to turn these ordinary pieces into an extraordinary dwelling in order to make the Tabernacle a place where Heaven meets earth. In verses 9-15, God requires Moses to anoint all the furniture and the entirety of the Tabernacle with oil. When oil is used in Scripture, it often symbolizes the power of Holy Spirit. As Moses spreads the oil, he is also setting the furniture apart as a sacred space, wholly dedicated to the Lord. Not only is Moses obedient in anointing the furniture, he also anoints Aaron and his sons, establishing and setting apart the priesthood line for generations to come.

Once Moses finished the work, "the cloud covered the tent of meeting, and the glory of the Lord filled the Tabernacle" (v.34). The cloud was a familiar sight for the Israelites who had witnessed it on Mount Sinai, and now God was able to consecrate the Tabernacle and be with His people in the closest possible way.

Despite the repeated failures of the Israelites and the overwhelming evidence of their sinful nature recorded throughout the book of Exodus, we consistently see God's faithful and loving character shine through. To God they are still His chosen people, and He wants to continue to set them apart, leading them into the land He had promised to Abraham, Isaac, and Jacob. He will be with them "in the sight of all the house of Israel throughout all their journeys" (v.38), just as He promised them on Mount Sinai when He established His covenant with them (Exodus 6:7). He pledged that He would be their God and Israel His people, and He demonstrates His faithfulness to them as He continually reveals more of Himself to the Israelites even when their character reveals divided hearts.

Like the Israelites, we, too, have been set apart and anointed with the power of Holy Spirit. Second Corinthians 1:21-22 promises, "Now He who establishes us with you in Christ and anointed us is God, who also sealed us and gave *us* the Spirit in our hearts as a pledge" (NASB). In Revelation 21:3, God also gives us the same assurance, "God's dwelling place is now among the people, and he will dwell with them. They will be his people, and God himself will be with them and be their God."

Even though, like the Israelites, we may not see God manifested in fire or a cloud to direct our ways, we have God's Word and Holy Spirit to guide us on our journey. We can also hold tightly to the truth that God is a faithful Promise-keeper who desires to be in relationship with us and will dwell amongst us once again. For when the glorious day comes when Jesus returns and there is a new Heaven and a new earth, the Lord God Almighty and the Lamb will be our temple (Revelation 21:22).

As we close the page on travelling with the Israelites, how is God inviting you to journey forward with Him? Thank Him for His faithful presence that has sustained you this far and allow it to propel you to confidently take your next step.

Contributing Writers

We are so grateful for our writing team and the heart and wisdom that they have brought to this project. Connect with them on Instagram to read more of their work.

Vickey Bentley	@purposeful_joy
Adéle Deysel	@adeledeysel
Ellie Di Julio	@elliedijulio
Kay Gleaves	@becomingkaygleaves
Shelley Johnson	@shelleylinnjohnson
Mazhar Kefali	@mazharkefali
Ashley Kelly	@rooted.and.strong
Jenna Marie Masters	@marked_by_love
Jeff McKee	@jeffmckeenz
Tabitha Meglich	@ajoyfulsparrow
Paula Morrison	@paula_morrison2804
Nicole O'Meara	@nicoleeomeara
Amber Palmer	@myjarsofclay
Emily Tyler	@helloemtyler
Aimée Walker	@aimeerwalker

About the Devoted Collective

Our vision is simple: to wholeheartedly pursue the 'more' of God together.

This looks like serving God with wholehearted devotion, fulfilling the command Christ gave us to love the Lord with all our heart, soul, and mind (Matthew 22:37).

We want to love God with all that we are right where we are. In order to do that, The Devoted Collective is anchored in three core disciplines modelled for us in Acts 2:42: devotion to the Word, to community, and to prayer. It is our heart's desire that, through committing to these practices with us, you will experience the richness of all God intends for your life as you come to know Him more intimately.

The more we know God, the more we can't help but love Him; and the more we love Him, the more we'll desire to partner with Him to establish it on earth as it is in Heaven. And that's what wholehearted devotion is all about. It's about living into the MORE of God.

Connect with us:

Website: www.thedevotedcollective.org
Socials: @thedevotedcollective

Join Us in the Devoted Community

We want to invite you to be part of The Devoted Community.

A curated online space hosted by Elim accredited Pastor Aimée Walker and Go + Tell Gals Certified Coach and Pastor, Em Tyler, The Devoted Community is an intentional discipleship hub, that will equip, empower, and release you into all that God has for you and help you build a resilient relationship with your God. It's where you'll find a company of women to cheer you on and a toolkit of resources to help you grow and go deeper with God.

WITHIN OUR COMMUNITY YOU WILL FIND:

Bible reading plans
Interviews & Teaching videos
Prayer threads and small groups
Dedicated mentors and monthly lives with Aimée and Emily
Access to our digital courses
Downloadable study guides & journals
Believers seeking the heart of God—just like you

WHO IS IT FOR?

If you are hungry and thirsty for more of Jesus. . .
If you desire to go deeper in your faith. . .
If you want to take hold of all the promises of God. . .
If you yearn for your faith to make a difference every day. . .
If you long to enjoy Him all the days of your life. . .
If you are looking for others who feel the same. . .

. . .then The Devoted Community is for you.

Let's pursue the MORE of God together:

www.thedevotedcollective.org/community

www.ingramcontent.com/pod-product-compliance
Lightning Source LLC
Chambersburg PA
CBHW051858090426
42811CB00003B/372